CREATING CONGREGATIONS OF GENEROUS PEOPLE

MICHAEL DURALL

AN ALBAN INSTITUTE PUBLICATION

Library of Congress Catalog Card Number 99-73552
ISBN 1-56699-220-6

To my wife, Diane, without whom

this book would never have been possible,

and to the brave souls who will lead pledge drives

in their own congregations

From Benjamin Franklin's *Autobiography and Other Writings*,
on hearing famed orator and evangelist George Whitefield.

*"I happened soon after to attend one of his sermons, in the course
of which I perceived he intended to finish with a collection,
and I silently resolved he should get nothing from me.
I had in my pocket a handful of copper money, three or four silver
dollars, and five pistoles in gold.*

*As he proceeded I began to soften and concluded to give the coppers.
Another stroke of his oratory made me ashamed of that
and determined me to give the silver;
and he finished so admirably that I emptied my pocket wholly into
the collector's dish, gold and all."*

CONTENTS

What This Book Is All About

A great deal of difference distinguishes asking people for money and creating congregations of generous people. Asking people for money eventually becomes routine, even tedious. But creating congregations of generous people is an engaging, rewarding endeavor that takes on ever more meaning with passing time.

Since you are reading this book, you probably wish to increase giving in your congregation, or you are seeking new ways to conduct the annual pledge drive. Secular organizations solicit financial support from members and friends, and many do so very effectively. But I believe religious organizations have a stronger authority—indeed, a moral authority—to challenge people to lead generous lives. As Robert Wood Lynn, independent consultant and retired Lilly Endowment executive, writes, "Churches should not be viewed as just another special interest group that asks for money."

People give more money to their places of worship than to any other organization. Dedicated churchgoers give to their congregations for decades on end, through good times and bad. They see ministers come and go, adjust to variations in worship, and as the years go by, accept all manner of changes, many of which they may not like. Yet large numbers of parishioners give generously their entire lives, until they draw their final breaths—and indeed after, as they often include churches and synagogues in their wills and estate plans.

But these are not the best of times for mainline traditions. Membership in mainline congregations has declined since the late 1950s. In addition, as a percentage of household income, charitable giving to churches has decreased during this period. In many congregations elderly members are among the highest donors, and their ranks are thinning. The somber titles of two recent books by noted authors illustrate this situation very clearly. The first is

Princeton University Professor Robert Wuthnow's *The Crisis in the Churches: Spiritual Malaise, Fiscal Woe.*[1] The second is Episcopal priest and Alban Institute founder Loren Mead's *Financial Meltdown in the Mainline?*[2]

If this book had a subtitle, it would be "Defying Trends." Low-level and same-level giving, unfortunately, is an established tradition in many congregations. Beyond the church's own four walls, the consumer-oriented society encourages not charitable giving but rather the accumulation of consumer goods. Entrenched giving habits and the desire to live affluent lives are two powerful forces clergy and lay leaders encounter in trying to create a congregation of generous people.

This book has three main purposes. First, it will help clergy, lay leaders, and people in the pews understand more fully the reasons why people give (or don't give) to their churches and synagogues. Second, this understanding will help build a foundation for thoughtful, effective, and consistent stewardship programs over the years—a departure from the "think up a new theme every year" approach common to many congregations.

Third, the book contains time-tested recommendations for conducting successful stewardship programs. It also identifies pitfalls that volunteers often encounter. One of my goals is to build confidence and enthusiasm in volunteers for leading stewardship initiatives, so that they will find the experience engaging and rewarding.

During the years that I've been helping churches and nonprofit agencies devise fund-raising plans, I've realized that clergy and lay leaders do not have sufficient information or training to lead stewardship efforts effectively. A recent stewardship survey conducted by the Christian Stewardship Association, an organization that monitors religious giving trends, supports this view, reporting that 75 to 90 percent of ministers and lay leaders said they needed professional stewardship training.[3]

Most denominations publish stewardship literature, but these materials alone do not equip lay committees to initiate and sustain long-term stewardship programs. Some churches send clergy or lay leaders to stewardship workshops or seminars. But the quality of stewardship training is inconsistent; and since lay leadership changes rapidly, even the most effective stewardship programs may have only a short-term effect.

This book offers an approach to stewardship that I believe has more staying power. It draws the best examples from the stewardship literature and practices of many denominations. To these, I have added ideas and approaches that I use successfully in my own stewardship work with congregations.

Since annual pledge drives are the most visible stewardship programs in most congregations, this book addresses these drives in some detail. This is not just a "how to ask for money" book, but rather one that examines how parishioners view the use of money in their lives. This knowledge is an essential element in understanding the culture of giving in congregations, and in discerning how charitable giving helps us grow in our religious faith.

In my view, the traditional pledge drive inadvertently reinforces low-level and same-level giving. Stewardship methods typically used in congregations actually limit the spiritual growth of members—often because pledge drives are conducted from the leadership down. The stewardship committee, with input from the minister and the church board, plans the drive and announces it to the congregation. The emphasis is usually on mechanics—the stewardship sermon, the pledge letters, the pulpit announcements.

This traditional approach manifests a significant shortcoming: It does not assess the attitudes of parishioners toward charitable giving. If clergy and lay leaders don't know how parishioners view the use of money in their lives, the leaders are at a disadvantage in asking them for it. A majority of congregants may, in fact, see no reason to increase their giving. The church eventually pays its bills, so what difference does it make? The traditional pledge drive does not address or challenge this widely held view. It allows parishioners to give very little for years on end.

This book recommends a "pews-up" approach based on significantly increased congregational ownership of the stewardship process. This approach does not mean discarding stewardship methods that congregations may be using successfully. Rather, the methods recommended can strengthen stewardship efforts already underway by helping leaders assess the attitudes of parishioners toward the use of money in their lives.

To what extent do parishioners view money as the means to a good life—expensive clothes, cars, homes, private schools, consumer goods, travel, and other trappings of an affluent society? To what extent do parishioners believe that sharing a larger portion of what they have been given is a core religious value, necessary to building a stronger faith?

Part I discusses how money is viewed in religious settings. We will examine views toward money ranging from "high-expectation" faith groups, which ask for a tithe (10 percent of income), to traditions that leave charitable decisions to members' discretion. These comparisons will help readers understand more fully the religious motivations to give, and where their congregations stand relative to other American faith communities.

Part II will help in planning and conducting more successful stewardship programs, and in establishing a more favorable climate of giving in the congregation. The recommendations are not specific formulas that need to be followed step by step. They are more like recipes, and various ingredients can be substituted to suit the tastes of a congregation's own giving tradition.

This book includes examples of stewardship programs conducted both effectively and poorly. These examples are illustrations to learn from; they show mistakes to avoid. Churches and synagogues are sometimes managed very poorly. Some congregations maintain organizational and managerial practices that would never be tolerated in the business world. Not uncommonly, ineffective stewardship practices put into effect years ago have been carried forward for no good reason, and are institutionalized in the life of the congregation. As we will see, many stewardship practices defy logic. They are often handed down to the next generation of unsuspecting stewardship volunteers.

We will also discuss the difference between stewardship and fundraising. Stewardship includes the ways we encourage people to lead generous lives, and how we use all the resources at our command to strengthen our religious faith and make the world a better place. This is the overriding concept of the book. In contrast, fund-raising includes the variety of methods we use to ask parishioners for money. Both stewardship and fund-raising require expertise, which I believe this book provides in good measure.

This book does not describe how to conduct a capital campaign. Also, it assumes that no crises of major proportion have erupted in the congregation within recent memory.

Creating a climate for increased generosity and raising money effectively over the long term are not easy tasks. They require patience, stamina, and persistence. Stewardship work also requires an understanding of why people come to church and how they construct religious lives for themselves and their families. This is fascinating work—God's work indeed, and our work too.

ACKNOWLEDGMENTS

I have been blessed by the helpful comments, thoughts, and suggestions of many people in writing this book. A special thanks goes to author and friend Jeff Bradley, who made the once-remote possibility of writing a book more plausible. Thanks also to my colleague Ellen Stevens, for her ongoing comments as the book progressed.

When I met with Robert Wood Lynn, he asked, "Why do you want to write a book?" At that time, I thought I knew the answer to that seemingly innocuous question, but I really didn't.

I am appreciative of the Rev. Victor Carpenter and the support provided by the Parish Committee and members of the First Church Unitarian Universalist in Belmont, Massachusetts. Thanks also to those who read chapters of the book in draft form. They include Cheryl Minor, David Williams, Robert Tobin, Denise Tracy, and Steve Knox.

I am indebted to the Rev. Carolyn Clarke for the strong direction of ministry that she related to me. Mark Chaves also added a perspective that I had not previously considered. Anyone who writes about church life also owes eternal gratitude to Lyle Schaller, Loren Mead, and Robert Wuthnow, who provide inspiration and guidance.

And finally, the staff of the Alban Institute has been extraordinarily professional and helpful. Acquisitions editor Beth Ann Gaede cheerfully and tirelessly separated a lot of chaff to find the wheat. Copy editor Jean Caffey Lyles did a careful and thoughtful reading. And editorial assistant Deborah Schnabel shepherded the book through various administrative procedures. You have all been just wonderful.

PART I

Raising Money in Religious Communities

CHAPTER 1

What Kind of People Do We Want to Become?

Do you remember those old-fashioned Popsicles, the ones with two wooden sticks? They were made so that kids could break a Popsicle in two and give half to a friend. Eating a whole one by yourself was never as much fun. As children, we were encouraged by our parents and other adults to share. We may not have wanted to; at times we may have been forced to. But in my childhood, being called "stingy" was a terrible insult. As adults, few of us would wish to be known as miserly, the grown-up equivalent of being a stingy child.

Throughout this book we'll discuss what makes some people generous and others less so, or not at all. I believe that being a generous person is one of life's great privileges. This is true whether we give money to churches and synagogues, or to colleges, museums, symphony orchestras, or other nonprofit organizations that enrich our lives.

The definition of generosity might also include sharing our time and talent with religious and secular organizations that help the less fortunate and strive to make the world a better place to live. Although such practices will not be addressed in this book, generosity could also encompass such issues as being hospitable, giving people the benefit of the doubt, practicing forgiveness, and manifesting other personal traits that characterize religious values and teachings.

Despite all the talk about and the actual practice of raising money in churches and synagogues, members of mainline traditions are rarely challenged to increased generosity. Many congregations, in fact, shy away from this approach. Church leaders often believe that asking people to increase their giving would offend them. Thus, many congregations accept small gifts from parishioners, usually in the form of weekly envelopes or through the annual pledge drive. Over time, congregations inadvertently reinforce the belief that giving little is acceptable. It is not uncommon for church leaders to believe that parishioners, despite outward signs of wealth, have little to give; or that parishioners are giving as much as they can, even if giving levels are low and no one knows what anyone else is contributing.

A commonly held belief among Christians is that the more one gives, the more one grows in faith. Unfortunately, the small-gift mentality that exists in many congregations diminishes people's capacity to grow spiritually in personal faith and to grow in character as human beings.

Such attitudes toward charitable giving create congregations that struggle each year to raise sufficient operating income. Low salaries for clergy, music directors, religious educators, and other church staff become the norm. A "We don't have the money" mentality all too easily takes up residence, crowding out a congregation's hopes and dreams. Church consultant Lyle Schaller writes that low-level giving creates a culture of scarcity that has even farther-reaching effects, "creating leaders who do not view their role as expanding ministry, but minimizing expenses."[1]

An important question about stewardship is, Should generosity be one of the core values of religious people? Phrased less delicately, is it possible to lead miserly lives (or conversely, lives of great indulgence) while giving little to the church or to any other charitable organization—yet attending worship services and considering oneself to be a person of faith?

What kinds of people do our churches and synagogues challenge us to become? Let's consider two views.

Varieties of Giving

In the Christian tradition, stewardship literature is often based on Scripture. In literature from the United Church of Christ, for example, parishioners are encouraged to "grow in Christ," or to become "spiritually mature" in their faith. Another recommendation is that people "examine their relationship to the Lord" to determine an appropriate gift.[2]

Charitable giving in the Jewish tradition is expressed differently through the concept of *tzedakah*, handed down from generation to generation. Translated from the Hebrew, *tzedakah* means "righteous giving," in which sharing is not a matter of individual preference, prayer, or reflection but rather a duty and an expectation, a matter of honor and justice. Many Jews believe that not giving would be like failing to provide for their children—an unthinkable dereliction.

One tradition describes giving as a matter of spiritual growth; the other as a matter of duty and righteousness. Though different, both are religious motivations based on one's relationship to the divine, made manifest in community. Both address the question, What kind of people are we, and what kind of people do we wish to become over the course of our lives?

Chapter 4, "What Can Churches Ask Parishioners to Give?" provides examples of how various denominations approach stewardship. Sometimes the motivation to give is based on Scripture, thankfulness, and reciprocity. At other times it grows from a sense of duty or a desire to make the world a better place for oneself and others. Denominations such as the Church of Jesus Christ of Latter-day Saints (Mormons) and the Assemblies of God are "high-expectation" or "high-demand" churches that expect members to tithe (give 10 percent of their incomes), usually as a *minimum*.

At the other end of the spectrum are congregations with few if any expectations about giving. These, including liberal denominations like the Unitarian Universalists, encourage parishioners to give but leave it to members themselves to determine the amount. Charitable giving is viewed as a matter of individual choice.

In mainline traditions, giving tends to be a matter of choice rather than of duty. Denominations and congregations approach the subject of charitable giving from different points of view, and people give or don't give for complex reasons. I believe congregations struggle to raise money because clergy and lay leaders do not sufficiently understand parishioners' attitudes toward the use of money in their lives, nor their giving intentions. Congregations ask for money, sometimes frequently, sometimes infrequently. Dollar goals may or may not be reached. But I believe that most religious communities don't understand fully how parishioners react to various appeals and why certain people respond generously and others not at all.

This book is written primarily for mainline Protestant congregations whose members are middle and upper-middle class. To be sure, some families and individuals in mainline churches experience financial hardship. But they do not ordinarily face poverty. They have adequate incomes to live relatively comfortable lives and have the means to make charitable gifts.

I believe congregations should recognize three issues that reflect the lives of contemporary churchgoers and their attitudes toward charitable giving.

1. Even if we have the money, we may wish to spend it on ourselves rather than give it away. In her well-researched book *The Overspent American*, Juliet Schor, an associate professor at the Harvard Business School,

reveals that the list of consumer items Americans believe they need grows ever longer and ever more expensive. Americans see or hear an estimated 38,000 advertisements for consumer products each year and are encouraged to buy what they want *now* or go into debt for it. Millions of families receive preapproved credit-card applications, many with special offers of free merchandise for those who open an account. This is heady competition for the traditional once-a-year stewardship sermon. The sad irony, according to Schor, is that Americans have more possessions than ever, yet feel poorer than ever. She writes: "By the mid-90s, countless Americans found themselves pessimistic, anxious, deprived or stuck, and spiritually bereft."[3]

Eileen Daspin, a writer for the *Wall Street Journal*, echoed this sentiment in an article titled "How to Give More." She writes:

> There is not a direct relationship between wealth and charity. During the stock market boom of the 1990s, proportionately fewer households gave to charity. The number of households making charitable gifts dropped from 71% to 68%. Those who still give are giving proportionately less, from 2.1% of personal income in 1967 compared to 1.6% in 1997. This is a 25% decrease, a significant percentage.[4]

Although income rose in the 1990s, charitable giving did not. This finding suggests that people were spending more on themselves. A meaningful theology of giving must acknowledge this reality.

The spending habits of churchgoing households are significant factors in their capacity and inclination to support the church financially. A growing number of congregations now offer financial-planning courses based on biblical principles to help members gain control over their personal finances, set spending priorities, and use charitable giving as a means of strengthening their religious faith. Scott Cormode, a professor at the Claremont School of Theology in California, says, "Until we can talk about things like how to pay the mortgage and how people can send their kids to a good school or have enough to help their parents get into a nursing home, we are not prepared to talk about giving."[5]

2. People sometimes become disillusioned with their churches or synagogues and believe them unworthy of support. For example, a minister or rabbi may leave or be asked to leave, with the incident undermining trust in religious leaders. Controversial issues such as gay and lesbian clergy, abortion, and biblical interpretation may alienate other members. Sometimes

parishioners get furious over the color of carpet selected for the sanctuary! Some problems begin with parishioners who bring unrealistic expectations. As with any close relationship, if parishioners believe the church or synagogue has failed them in some fundamental way, the hurt can be deep and long-lasting. People might leave their religious homes for short periods or for many years, not to return until the hurt has subsided, if ever. Others may turn their volunteer time and financial support to secular organizations, seeking meaning and involvement in their lives outside organized religion.

Parishioners' attitudes toward their congregations or denominations are subject to wide fluctuations. Parishioners may go through periods of confusion and despair about what they believe God's work to be and how the human institution of the church carries out that work—or fails to do so. As a result, their charitable giving may be affected significantly. A theology of giving cannot assume that parishioners feel loyal to the church and its mission or even connected to a particular congregation or denomination.

3. The third issue about money and giving is the religious belief that everything we have comes from God. Younger people today, many of whom were raised in unchurched households, do not believe in God's benevolence to us. Older generations, those who place greater value in the institutional church, may feel a duty to return some of God's many blessings. But their grandchildren may not feel that way at all. Tom Beaudoin, a 29-year-old divinity-school graduate, writes in his book *Virtual Faith: The Irreverent Spiritual Quest of Generation X*: "Many of us are at arm's length from religious institutions, even those of us who attend services regularly. We think that many of life's most religious experiences happen outside religious institutions and official worship services."[6]

Older generations may respond to traditional, biblically based appeals for charitable support. But younger generations, according to researchers Dean Hoge, Patrick McNamara, and Charles Zech,

> cannot be expected to respond to appeals for giving based on strong faith, or in the teachings of the Old and New Testaments. They are little different from secular people in how they think about monetary gifts. They are not motivated by promises of reciprocity with God.[7]

Thus, the traditional theme of the year and the one-size-fits-all pledge drive fail to encompass wide-ranging beliefs across the generations about how we grow in faith and character, our role in accomplishing the church's mission, and the reasons we give. As Beaudoin explains, "The old way in which religious institutions related to people of faith with a paternalistic, condescending set of assumptions should no longer exist."[8] I believe that charitable giving in mainline faiths has decreased for the past 30 years because congregations and denominations have failed to recognize the increasing complexity of modern life and to develop a theology of giving that fits these realities.

Congregants hold a wondrous array of theological beliefs. If their attitudes toward the use of money in their lives can be determined, it should be possible to reshape stewardship programs into more thoughtful, intelligent, engaging, theological, and practical enterprises. Such programs will have a greater chance of long-term success and, most important, strengthen people of all ages in their religious faith.

Anthony Pappas, author of numerous books about life in small churches, challenges his readers to consider, "Who should we become in order to fulfill God's destiny for us in this place and time?"[9] Rephrasing this question in a charitable context, we might ask, "How should we use all the resources at our command, both in our individual lives and in congregations, to become more generous people and thus fulfill God's destiny and accomplish God's design for this world?"

Helping people lead more generous lives is one of the themes we will explore in this book. Like much work of faith, changing people's minds about becoming more generous will not be easy. Congregations have created some obstacles for themselves around which we can maneuver. Other obstacles affect almost all mainline congregations nationwide and may be difficult if not impossible to overcome.

The jury is still out on whether congregations can reverse the trend of low-level and same-level giving, and on the extent to which congregations can challenge members to seek alternatives to the prevailing consumer culture. There is much work to be done. In the premier issue of *Stewardship Matters* magazine, Tom McCabe (editor of *Inside Outreach: A Guide to Financing Christian Outreach Ministries*) suggests that "people who help raise money for their churches may be God's messengers to His people regarding His will for them in giving."[10]

When I took on a stewardship role in my own congregation, I didn't view myself as God's messenger. I thought my job was to raise money for the church; i.e., fund-raising. Once involved, however, I was surprised at how engrossed I became in the stewardship process, and the powerful sense of ownership that ensued. I felt my congregation wasn't engaged sufficiently in the stewardship conversation—there was so much to discuss and to learn. It has been a wonderful experience for me, and I hope it will be for you, too.

CHAPTER 2

The Typical Pledge Drive, Alas!

Most congregations conduct their annual pledge drive as a kind of sales pitch, geared to meet the church's operating budget. The pledge committee is often a group of dedicated though reluctant souls who are viewed as having gotten stuck with the church's most unenviable job.

The Pitch

Very likely, the pledge committee is new to the task and has received little, if any, orientation or training. Its role, more or less, is to devise a theme and persuade the congregation to give money to the church. Pledge drives, depending on the nature of individual churches, contain references to Scripture, a bit of humor, some good-natured cajoling, an appeal to the conscience, and a hint of guilt.

I do not recommend wholesale abandonment of the annual pledge drive. I do believe, however, that traditional methods used to conduct pledge drives inadvertently create and perpetuate a small-gift mentality in religious communities. The typical pledge drive can also be disheartening, if not downright distressing, for pledge-drive volunteers.

For definition's sake, the annual pledge drive is the way churches raise unrestricted operating income each year. The annual fund pays for things like salaries, heat and lights, insurance, and other fixed costs. The annual fund is the congregation's checking account. Money that comes in is usually spent the same year. Some congregations make the annual operating budget available for all to see, while others do not or share only certain portions. For example, some congregations do not disclose salary figures, or list only the combined salaries of all paid staff.

The annual pledge drive also does not include capital campaigns, which are usually launched for larger goals, spread over longer periods of time, and earmarked for specific purposes such as new construction or building renovations. Nor does the annual pledge drive include appeals for hunger, disaster relief, or other special causes.

Some congregations ask parishioners to make an annual pledge, the total amount they intend to give for the coming year. Parishioners then pay their pledges in a variety of ways—a weekly offering, a monthly check, or a quarterly or semiannual payment. It is not uncommon for congregations in affluent areas to receive one check for the entire amount. Many congregations ask parishioners for a weekly amount and provide envelopes for the collection plate. This weekly practice reinforces the belief that giving is an integral part of the worship experience. These are not mutually exclusive practices. Congregations request and receive financial support from members in many ways.

In many congregations the operating budget is the centerpiece of the annual pledge drive. Sometimes parishioners are offered a choice of more than one budget. Three choices seem to be popular. These include the basic model that is about the same as last year's budget, a slightly increased version, and a "stretch" budget that contains new programs or initiatives.

As the pledge drive gets underway, the first step in many congregations is to send a stewardship letter to members and friends. In some congregations a pledge card is included with the letter, and in others it is mailed later, distributed before or after worship services, or carried along on home visits. In many congregations, the same letter is sent to every household, including those that have given the most and those that haven't given at all. In some congregations, the minister, rabbi,[1] members of the stewardship committee, or members of the congregation pay stewardship visits to people's homes. Whichever method is used, the pledge committee anxiously awaits the results.

The Response

A small band of generous souls heeds the call and returns pledge cards right away. These pledges (and sometimes checks for the full or a partial amount) are likely to come from parishioners who already pledge the most. Many of these high-level donors will increase their pledges. Among this group one may occasionally find a same-level pledge, but rarely will a pledge be less than in previous years. If a pledge is less, the pledge card will probably be accompanied by a note of explanation or apology. This stalwart group can be relied upon for its financial support year in and year out. Among these pillars are a few people in their 70s and 80s, often the largest donors in the congregation. The pledge committee is heartened to see the drive get off to a good start.

A more sizable segment of the congregation takes longer, much longer, to ponder what to give. It may be simple procrastination, or people may have misplaced their pledge cards. Weeks pass. Announcements and heartrending testimonials about the meaning of the church in our lives are made each Sunday from the pulpit. Notices appear in the church newsletter. Pledges trickle in.

The pledge committee begins to think about sending a follow-up letter and, horror of horrors, having to telephone those who have not pledged. Clergy and lay leaders begin wondering if they should plan a contingency budget, one that contains some cuts.

After four or five weeks of pulpit announcements and newsletter updates, the pledge message becomes intrusive, and parishioners grow tired of hearing about it. Morale wanes.

Those who give the least add to the suspense by delaying the longest to make their pledges. When they get follow-up letters or phone calls, some complain that "all the church ever talks about is money." In some congregations, the pledge drive can drag on for months, during which time those who have pledged are continually reminded of those who have not. This practice is disheartening to those who made their gifts or pledges early. Haranguing nondonors from the pulpit or writing repeated pleas in the church newsletter should be discouraged at all costs—the nondonors are those who attend church least and probably don't read the newsletter, either. The pleas do not reach the intended audience.

A helpful model of church participation (and an accurate reflection of charitable giving) is one described to me by David Williams, a minister in the United Church of Christ. It is a pie chart formulated by Stephen Gray, a ministerial colleague. A very small slice, about 5 percent of the pie, is the church leadership. A second slice, about 20 percent of the members, constitutes the pillars. These two groups make up the core of the church community, ever-reliable in terms of what needs to be done at church.

They also provide the largest gifts. Look to these groups when you need help and support of any kind.

The third slice of the pie is about 25 percent. These are the people who are "present." They attend worship services and various events and may contribute a modest amount, but in general they do not take on leadership roles or stand out.

The final and largest slice of the pie, unfortunately, is the remaining half. These members are inert. In some congregations they are described by the oxymoron "inactive members." They may show up on Christmas and Easter, or on other special occasions. One may well wonder whether church has any effect on their lives at all. The church gets low-level or token gifts from this group. Gray suggests that capital campaigns sometimes stimulate inert members to come forward with significant gifts because they wish to preserve a building that holds great meaning. I'm skeptical myself.

Completing the Pledge Drive

Eventually, the pledge committee concludes the visible part of the pledge drive with a sigh of relief. The pulpit announcements, reminders, various pleadings and coaxings come to an end. (In one congregation I recently visited, a pledge-drive leader referred to the conclusion of the pledge drive as "calling off the bloodhounds.") In congregations that are relatively stable, the basic budget, give or take a few dollars, is usually reached. Rarely do congregations meet the slightly increased budget, and almost never the "stretch" budget, even though that goal may have been only slightly higher. Sometimes a congregation will reach a higher goal one year, then shrink back to previous giving habits.

In tallying the figures, clergy and lay leaders will find that most parishioners gave about the same as the previous year—or the previous ten years. Low-level and same-level giving raises an issue: If giving remains the same, do other aspects of a person's relationship with the congregation and with God also remain the same? Does a person's or family's worship attendance change? Do personal or family spiritual practices remain unchanged? Do commitments to ministry both inside and outside the congregation remain the same? Does a person or family grow in faith from year to year? Or, regrettably, does the church have little effect on their lives?

Some members of the pledge committee are discouraged that after all the time and effort they invested, the congregation didn't respond more positively to the message or rise to the occasion. They want the job over and done with. Many vow never to do it again. In a few extreme cases, volunteers find the experience so distressing that they leave the church.

The sad irony is that congregations are usually unaware of low- and same-level giving, because pledge committees are reluctant to say that things are not going well. As a result, poor giving habits and the difficulty of conducting a pledge drive are subjects rarely discussed. Poor giving habits and customs are perpetuated from year to year, lying in wait for the next group of unsuspecting pledge-drive volunteers. And few in the church give much thought to whether people are growing in faith.

Reporting the Results

Once the pledge drive has concluded, the pledge committee has one more task. It needs to announce the results to the congregation. Some churches report only the total raised. A more common practice is reporting three figures to the congregation. The first two are the total amount pledged and the number of pledging households. The third is the average (mean) pledge, which in most congregations ranges from $200 to $850 per year, or between $4 and $17 per week.

Calculating the average pledge, a commonsense idea, in fact grossly distorts pledge-drive results. It is also patently unfair. When only the average pledge is calculated, the generous are perceived as giving less, while those who give the least are viewed as giving considerably more.

This perception, of course, is the opposite of how it should be. This approach creates churches that author Ashley Hale describes as chapters of the BPATG—The Benevolent and Protective Association of Token Givers.[2]

In many congregations the pledge drive is cloaked in secrecy. Reporting only the average pledge fosters the notion that everyone in the pews gives about the same amount. The truth is that in almost all congregations, one-third of the households give two-thirds or more of the total. This proportion is considered a sign of a financially healthy congregation, by the way. But most congregations do not communicate this fact to the membership, often for the simple reason that pledge committees don't do calculations beyond the total amount pledged and the average pledge.

One additional aspect of this system allows generous donors to remain unrecognized and protects those who give little. In many instances, clergy believe that only the treasurer should know what people give to the church. In some congregations, this policy is written into the bylaws. The reasoning is that if clergy knew how much people gave to the church, they would practice favoritism toward those who give the most—usually assumed to be the wealthiest families.

When Martin Luther King, Sr., assumed the leadership of Ebenezer Baptist Church in Montgomery, Alabama, in the 1930s, he ended the long-held tradition of secrecy surrounding what people gave to the church. He opened the pledge records of the church for anyone to see. Anonymous gifts would be accepted but not recorded. "The practice of anonymous giving," he thundered from the pulpit, "leads to the practice of anonymous non-giving!"[3]

Clergy are sometimes taught in seminary that a person's gift should be known only to God. But this precept also means that clergy are unaware of and unable to acknowledge families of modest means who contribute in comparable proportion to, or even greater proportion than, wealthier families. Statistical evidence indicates that people of modest means give in equal proportion to or sometimes greater proportion than those with more wealth.[4] In congregations that promote secrecy, the opportunity is lost to acknowledge and thank parishioners, both rich and poor, who give generously. In my own work with churches, I have found that the higher the level of secrecy, the lower the level of giving.

Keeping the giving records secret also creates difficulties for volunteers who conduct the annual pledge drive. They don't know how much to ask people for. This is one way in which the traditional pledge drive reinforces same-level giving from year to year. I am familiar with congregations in which treasurers or financial secretaries have kept pledge figures secret for years, threatening to resign in protest if they are asked to divulge the numbers. While well-intentioned, these people do great harm, holding congregations hostage because of poorly thought-out practices and outworn customs.

Church consultant Loren Mead writes:

> Such campaigns limp along from year to year. That such a haphazard system generates billions in gifts each year is astonishing. It makes churches the envy of all other nonprofits. People must want to give to their churches if they give with so little encouragement. Yet I contend that this strategy is inadequate.[5]

If little thought is given to reporting financial-giving figures, even less energy is devoted to reporting other indices of the congregation's spiritual well-being. These include attendance at worship, the number of people involved in education programs, and the hours spent volunteering. Is it any wonder that if churches cannot report how people grow in faith, they cannot persuade people to increase their giving?

Stewardship Literature: Sometimes Helpful, Sometimes Not

In their efforts to assist congregations, most denominations publish materials that recommend various stewardship strategies. These books, pamphlets, videos, and flyers fall into two general categories. The first is the "call forth" approach. These materials are usually biblically based and inspirational. They appeal to our sense of God's blessing and call us to return in some measure that which we have been given. This literature appeals on an emotional level and inspires us to our highest calling. Included in this category is mission-based giving, or calls to expand the realm of God. Congregants are asked to pray about their commitment and to refer to Scripture and other readings for examples and inspiration.

The second category is the more practical "how-to" stewardship resource. These materials focus on management of the pledge drive and emphasize setting up committees and leadership structures. Some propose simple approaches, others more complex programs. A stewardship guide from the Unitarian Universalists, for example, recommends organizing nine separate committees. Suggested committees include executive, advance gifts, leadership gifts, general canvass, administrative, treasury, kickoff, communications, and continuing/follow-up.[6]

While these materials can be helpful, the "call forth" approach based on Scripture does not often resonate with younger churchgoers. Consultant Robert Wood Lynn summarizes this point succinctly by noting, "What appeals to one generation can wear thin in the next. So the search for authoritative arguments continues in every era."[7]

The "how to" materials, in turn, are often lengthy, posing a daunting task to newly recruited volunteers. Even the two categories of materials used in combination do not provide volunteers sufficient instruction to conduct effective stewardship programs. Both types of stewardship materials also tend to portray parishioners and churches as basically alike and offer a "one-size-fits-all" model.

I believe both the "call forth" and the "how to" approaches, useful as they can be, overlook a number of important issues that affect charitable giving in religious communities—both in the life of the congregation as a whole, and in the lives of individual parishioners. There are three issues to consider:

1. *People give for different reasons.* Unfortunately, most pledge drives are not based on the heartfelt reasons people give. The "theme of the year" approach may in fact speak to only a small segment of the congregation. Thus, for many parishioners the pledge drive is a forgettable event in the church calendar rather than an opportunity to grow in faith.

I believe the pledge drive should be at the core of congregational life, an integral part of supporting the mission of the congregation and what it is called to do in the world. The pledge drive should challenge the congregation in many thoughtful, engaging ways. For those of more traditional religious beliefs, the pledge drive should contain references to Scripture, stressing the opportunity to meditate and pray about how God has blessed us, how we desire to show our gratitude in return, and how we can grow in our spiritual lives.

For those who may not find Scripture a motivation to give, the pledge drive can appeal as an investment in making the world a better place to live, helping the less fortunate, taking greater ownership and involvement in a particular project, or becoming a meaningful part of a meaningful organization. For yet others, the challenge should be a matter of building character—what kind of people do we wish to become? The pledge drive in today's church needs to be multifaceted, to reach all segments of the community.

Of course, none of these approaches is mutually exclusive and in fact should be complementary. People in the pews, as they grow in age and in faith, will have changing views. Their spiritual lives may deepen. Their financial circumstances may change, gradually or dramatically, for better or for worse. As a pledge-drive volunteer, you may find yourself wishing that parishioners would learn the stewardship lesson once and for good. It seems so simple. A friend of mine, a bishop of the Mormon Church (a tithing denomination), once said to me, "I don't understand why you have to convince members to support the church over and over again, year after year. Why don't they just give what they know they are supposed to?" But the reality for mainline churches today is decreased giving and a high rate of same-level giving.

2. *Congregations are alike, yet different.* In his book *The Middle-Sized Church*, Lyle Schaller, an expert on congregational issues, writes that

churches of the same denomination, even if they are in the same community, can be surprisingly different from one another. "No two churches are alike," he writes.[8] It is likely that no two pledge drives are alike either. Yet a great deal of stewardship literature tends to treat congregations as basically the same. The history and tradition of a congregation, along with the community in which it is located, are factors that will significantly affect the outcome of a pledge drive.

For example, some congregations are growing in membership, while others are declining. Small congregations are different from large ones. Neighborhoods vary. Some congregations have histories of strong clergy or lay leadership, while others have troubled histories, creating a lack of trust among parishioners. No single "how to" or "call forth" approach can possibly meet the variety of issues that congregations face in seeking financial support from their members.

Let me provide two examples of how pledge drives vary from congregation to congregation. I know of a minister called to a small church. On a Sunday morning about halfway through his first year, a member of the board strode to the lectern and announced that the pledge drive had been successfully completed. The minister hadn't even known it was underway!

I encountered the opposite approach in a mid-sized church, in which a highly regarded parishioner recruited almost half the congregation to be involved in the pledge drive. Each volunteer was required to ask just one other member of the congregation for a pledge. In contrast to the stealth approach noted above, recruiting almost half the membership was highly visible in the congregation.

3. *Just as people change, so do religious communities.* Whenever a new minister or rabbi is called, some people leave, newcomers join, and others who left years before may drift back. Sometimes people get angry at their church or synagogue, and leave or withhold financial support. Sometimes a charismatic religious leader brings rapid growth to a congregation, creating a variety of growing pains. Or the reverse, a popular religious leader leaves, and a once-large congregation begins to lose membership. The pledge drive needs to address and reflect significant changes in the life of the congregation in an honest and straightforward manner. Generic pledge-drive themes like "Living in Harmony" are lackluster and do not address the reality and the urgency, immediacy, and importance of doing God's work in the world.

Also Note Well

Fund-raising does not come naturally. Most people do not like asking others for money—at church or anywhere else. A common refrain in congregations and nonprofit agencies is "I'll do anything but ask for money." Some people rank asking for money high on the most-feared list, right up there with public speaking.

With a large number of parishioners uninterested in assuming stewardship roles and a tendency for high turnover in pledge-drive volunteers, congregations often have difficulty recruiting strong leadership. In many congregations, leadership turns over every year. Clergy with whom I have spoken feel fortunate if pledge-drive leaders stay for two years. Beyond the issue of asking for money, volunteers usually do not stay because trying to persuade recalcitrant members to turn in their pledges is discouraging. If a congregation has difficulty recruiting people to lead the pledge drive, special efforts will be needed to make the job more attractive.

Leadership is the key to creating a climate for giving. Successful pledge drives require hearty souls who believe the money is out there, and that the more people give, the more they will grow in their spiritual lives. Pledge-drive leaders need to be enthusiastic about their role in the congregation. They need ample doses of persistence, stamina, patience, and determination to see the job through.

Stewardship volunteers also need to understand that the annual pledge drive is a ministry, a means by which the congregation can most frequently and consistently articulate the aspects of charitable giving that enhance our spiritual lives. Thus, the annual pledge drive requires dedicated, committed, skilled, well-trained, and consistent leadership. Your church should devote adequate time, financial support, and volunteer resources to developing leaders who will be able to conduct effective pledge drives each year. There is too much at stake to do otherwise.

The annual pledge drive is a challenge that requires intelligence and insight, a knowledge of how churches function, hard work, and a thick skin. But running the pledge drive can also be an engaging intellectual exercise in determining why people join religious organizations, what they find of meaning there, and why they support the work of the congregation.

Leading the pledge drive should be inspiring to clergy, lay leaders, and the congregation. The annual pledge drive, well-conducted, should be as important and meaningful as any other aspect of church life.

CHAPTER 3

Identifying and Overcoming Obstacles to Stewardship

The recent book *Financing American Religion*,[1] coedited by Mark Chaves and Sharon Miller, reveals the giving patterns of American churchgoers. We will take a look at one key issue, referred to as "skewed giving."

Skewed Giving

Skewed giving happens when a small number of donors contributes a disproportionately large share of the total. Skewed giving is a well-known and established fact in religious and secular organizations and not a new finding in *Financing American Religion*. However, understanding the concept is an important starting place in determining the giving patterns in a congregation.

In most congregations, 80 percent of donors give only about 20 percent of the total amount raised. This is called "the 80-20 rule." (Some denominational officials now suggest that a 90-10 rule is evolving.) In my own congregation, 11 percent of donors give almost half the total, and a 70-30 percentage applies to the congregation as a whole. Calculating these percentages in a congregation is an important starting point in determining the giving patterns of parishioners.

Beyond the 80-20 rule, researchers have found that giving patterns from denomination to denomination vary significantly only among the top 20 percent of donors.[2] Thus, the best chance of increased giving is among the top 20 percent of current donors. Many church volunteers with whom I have worked are hesitant to ask higher-level donors for larger gifts, but that is where the greatest potential lies.

People who are charitably inclined derive great satisfaction from giving, and few donors will give more than they can afford. Top donors could contribute substantially more if they wanted to, either to the church or to other organizations. Don't be afraid to ask!

How Skewed Giving Affects Stewardship

The principle of skewed giving may be familiar to many readers. However, the researchers for *Financing American Religion* point to two findings that stewardship volunteers should be aware of in planning stewardship programs. First, a large number of donors in the bottom 80 percent cannot articulate why they give at the level they do. Many respondents to surveys said they had given the same amount to the church for years but didn't know why they gave that amount, or how they decided to give it in the first place.[3]

Second, and most significant to pledge-drive volunteers: Even though donors in the bottom 80 percent cannot articulate why they give the amount they do, they are firmly resistant to increasing their giving levels. As coeditor Mark Chaves states, "Religious giving does not, in general, respond either to increased programming or to explicit appeals for individuals to rethink their giving levels."[4]

The hard lesson for pledge-drive volunteers is that attempts to increase the giving level of the bottom 80 percent of the congregation may be futile. In my own experience as a pledge-drive leader, I have resisted accepting this probability. Instead, when I began serving as a stewardship volunteer, I believed that a better pledge publication, more compelling appeals, and the professionalism I brought to the job would sway people's hearts and pocketbooks. It made a difference the first year, and 73 percent of members increased their pledges. Overall, our congregation experienced a 25 percent increase in giving, and we were thrilled. Our congregation was able to hire a student minister and a part-time youth advisor, both of whom added greatly to the life of the congregation. Since everything looked rosy and we had barely tapped the congregation's giving potential, we expected an increase the following year, too. Our congregation was receiving more, so we assumed members would give more.

The next year we raised the same amount of money, but from 10 percent fewer pledging households. About one-third of the congregation gave more, one-third renewed at the same level, and an increasing number became nonpledgers, including more than half of new members. It didn't make sense that a smaller number of households was giving more, that the number of same-level gifts had increased, and that the number of nonpledging families had risen. The congregation had faced no major crises or issues over these two years, and the region's economy remained strong. (I have since found this pattern in two other congregations of different sizes and denominations.)

I include this personal example to show that even after my many years in fund-raising, the results of the pledge drive in my own congregation are confusing. We are now trying to determine why giving differed so strikingly from one year to the next. Some families whose children are active in church did not renew their pledges. Others who are active in adult programs and who appear satisfied with the church continued to give minimal amounts. We suspect that a growing number of parishioners are loyal to a particular program, to music or education or outreach, but are not participants in worship or other aspects of the religious community as a whole. We also suspect that a consumer mentality has become part of church life, that people expect to receive benefits from the church at a low "cost" and don't believe they need to give more. Why pay more for something that already costs little or nothing? At this point, we have encouraged the board to appoint an ad-hoc committee to help determine and interpret attitudes toward giving among parishioners.

People give or don't give for complex reasons. These reasons may be difficult to discern, and may be unpredictable from year to year. In my congregation, some members believe we should call nondonors and ask more forcefully for money. Others believe that this practice is inappropriate and suggest that nondonors should simply be asked why they don't give. Still others think that any attempt to contact nondonors is an invasion of privacy.

My experience in working with congregations reflects research findings that additional programming and appeals to increase giving have little effect. People give what they give, sometimes with little rhyme or reason. In the eyes of stewardship volunteers, parishioners' giving may have little to do with what happens in church, or how the pledge drive is conducted.

One minister I know performed both a wedding and a memorial service for a family within a 12-month period. Both were large events and required a great deal of time and effort on the part of the congregation. This family also had a child in high school who had been in trouble and was helped greatly by the church's youth minister. Yet this family, which displayed many outward signs of wealth, steadfastly refused to give to the church. When asked by the stewardship chair to support the work of the congregation, the response was, "We'll think about it." They continued to be a noncontributing family.

This family may be an extreme example, but the attitude may be more prevalent than one would expect. Stewardship volunteers may be angered or disappointed by people who take blatant advantage of the church. For a certain segment of the congregation, however, literally nothing anyone can say or do will make any difference in their level of giving.

Teaching Generosity

Can generosity be taught? The answer to this engaging question has been addressed by Laurent Parks Daloz, a writer and cofounder of the Community College of Vermont. Daloz surveyed more than 100 people who worked for the common good, often in the face of complex and daunting circumstances.

Daloz sought to learn what kinds of experiences increased the probability that a person would live a life of commitment to a larger whole, and the factors that fostered a greater generosity of spirit in society. His findings provide insight into how religious institutions might engage congregants in the conversation about generosity in our lives.

Daloz found that several factors appear significant in the first three decades of a person's life. Not all appear in every life, and no single one is determinative. They are:

- The experience of being "seen" as a child
- Having at least one publicly active parent
- Growing up in a home that is hospitable to the wider world
- Living in a safe yet diverse neighborhood
- Actively participating in a religious life
- Having contact with adults in the community who model commitment
- Participating in youth groups
- Having mentors[5]

Where to Go from Here?

In identifying and overcoming obstacles to stewardship, two important issues merit our attention: What is your church like, and for what does it want to raise money? Stewardship is not separate from the ongoing life of the congregation; it mirrors congregational life as a whole. For example, if people come to church out of routine or habit and have low expectations of what the church can accomplish or how their lives will be changed, then stewardship initiatives will reflect these attitudes. You cannot take a congregation that is somnolent for 11 months of the year and make the members wildly enthusiastic about giving during the 12th.

Other congregations create and sustain the belief that they can accomplish anything they set out to do. In his wonderful book *Acting on Your Faith: Congregations Making a Difference*, author and social scientist Victor Claman reveals an inspiring array of programs and services that churches and synagogues of all sizes have begun.[6] These projects range in size from planting small gardens and raising animals in rural areas, to starting banks and large social-service agencies in urban areas. In literally every instance, regardless of program costs or geographic locale, congregations echoed the same sentiment—the money was usually there. Congregations included in the book tended to believe that if the Lord calls, the Lord provides.

What Is the Metaphor for Your Church?

Let's take a look at a few different congregations, to compare and contrast congregational life and giving patterns. "I'd describe my congregation as an old shoe," said Jonathan Taylor, pastor of a 450-member congregation. "The church is located in an affluent community with a stable population. Young families move here because of excellent public schools and stay for many years. The church is a familiar place. We spruced up the parlor and the bathrooms ten years ago, but nothing substantive has changed in the building since the 1920s.

"A member of the church who is the campaign chair for a large nonprofit agency led the pledge drive last year," Taylor continued, "and we went over the goal. Part of the reason we succeeded is that we are a low-pledging congregation and the capacity to give is tremendous. Church members are enlightened by my sermons, I hope, and enjoy our stunning choir.

They may think and feel certain things about religion, but parishioners don't view church as changing their lives in a substantive way. Parishioners lead comfortable lives by and large, and don't feel compelled to change things either at church or in the world. I don't think launching new initiatives and asking people to pay for them through the pledge drive would work because congregants don't want to do that in the first place."

"My church is just the opposite," said Maureen Clark, another pastor. "I'd characterize it as a congregation that requires a lot of hard work from the minister and staff. In fact, this is my fifth ministry, and it is the most difficult I've ever had. A metaphor would be the church as a treadmill. The church is located in a racially and economically mixed community near a major university. Unlike [Taylor's] congregation with its stable membership, we have high turnover, some students and a lot of visiting faculty. Leadership is a big problem. We are more outreach-oriented, as needy people and difficult situations present themselves literally at our doorstep.

"But with high turnover, it is just about impossible to get programs going and sustained. I ended up being a co-leader of the pledge drive because no one else would do it, and even though there is money in this congregation, we fell short of our goal. A strong belief is that people don't have money to give, which is not the case at all. But that's how we operate, just barely getting by. I'm an ex-officio member of just about every committee, coaxing and prodding people to keep involved, to keep going in spite of many obstacles. It is not exactly a crisis mentality, but I often feel that if I don't keep things going, everything will just stop. If we raised more money through the pledge drive, it would be easier on everyone, but I just don't see that happening."

These two congregations are of the same denomination and are located in adjacent communities less than two miles apart.

In talking with ministers about their congregations, I asked them to think of metaphors for their churches. I was quite taken with the metaphors they chose. An "old shoe" church. A "treadmill" church. Others described their churches in vivid ways. "A hostel by the side of the road," said a Presbyterian minister from a church in an economically depressed area, adding, "We never know who will show up, or how difficult their situation will be when they arrive."

A member of an inner-city Lutheran church that assists low-income people in the neighborhood described her congregation as "a candle, burning quietly, sometimes intense." An Episcopal rector in a quiet suburban town said, "When I think of my church, hobbits, the characters in [English writer] J. R. R. Tolkien's books, come to mind. Our building is earth-colored, with moss on the roof. We are close to the ground, comfortable in our smallness." One observer suggested that the metaphor for a nondenominational megachurch with 10,000 members was "a cup of designer coffee with lightning bolts coming out of it."

A minister with the United Church of Christ offered yet another metaphor for his congregation. "This congregation struggles with stewardship because we have a large endowment," he said. "People in my church don't think we need the money. . . . The metaphor here is that our church is a bank."

Clergy, boards of trustees, and pledge-drive leaders need to understand the metaphor of their own congregations to initiate and maintain effective stewardship programs. What is the metaphor for your church? What does your congregation stand for? What is it called to do? What does your congregation accomplish through the financial support that members provide?

Does Money Follow Mission?

Author and church consultant Kennon Callahan, in his book *Giving and Stewardship in an Effective Church*, writes, "Mission is more important than money. A clear vision of mission will be decisive in fostering your congregation's capacity for giving."[7] In my consulting work I have found a wide acceptance of the dictum that money follows mission. That is, if a congregation sets hopes, dreams, and goals for the future, parishioners will be inspired to give toward what the church wants to accomplish.

However, the research cited in *Financing American Religion* indicates that increased programming (expanding the mission) will not motivate 80 percent of the members of most congregations. This large group might believe that if the church does more, it will cost more, and they will be asked to pay more. This may not be an appealing option. I am familiar with a number of congregations in which parishioners believe the church already has enough money, maybe even too much. To give more would be financially imprudent, even foolish. How many people in your congregation might hold this view?

Theologian Douglas John Hall, in his widely read book *The Steward: A Biblical Symbol Come of Age*, also questions the notion of expanded mission, and in fact articulates the fallacy of money following mission. "Stewardship has been relegated to a strictly operational status," he writes. "It has become the term associated with little more than church management and finances, the acquisition of ecclesiastical monies and property."[8] Instead, Hall states emphatically, charitable giving should be the ultimate goal. He writes, "Stewardship itself should represent the summing up of a Christian life."[9]

In other words, Hall suggests that stewardship should not be viewed as giving money so that the church can do something with it. Rather, giving is to God. This is a view frequently held by members of the Assemblies of God. Assembly members give to God, and what the church does with the money is largely irrelevant. While I believe this view is sound in theory, for mainline congregations to adopt it would require a significant leap of faith among parishioners, a leap too far for many.

Nevertheless, I do believe the view that many people give directly to God is one that should be introduced in mainline congregations. For example, I used the Assemblies of God as an example of generosity on a stewardship Sunday in my own congregation. Some parishioners reacted with disbelief. They had never heard of high-expectation giving before, and were stunned that Assembly members would make personal and financial sacrifices to practice their faith. To me, stewardship education should provide insights into the charitable behavior of many religious traditions, particularly those that vary dramatically from one's own.

I believe that stewardship initiatives in the congregation should include a clarification of the mission—accomplishing the work of God. Stewardship efforts should also be a means by which parishioners strengthen their faith. How a congregation views these issues will change from year to year. The concepts of mission and money are ones a congregation needs to discuss, debate, pray about, and face squarely to create and sustain a congregation of generous people.

In attempting to strengthen both faith and mission among members of the congregation, keep in mind a finding from *Financing American Religion*. Parishioners who give the least are motivated by maintaining the building and the congregation. More generous parishioners believe they are also helping people who are less fortunate, and strengthening their relationship to God.[10] What do members of your congregation believe, and how will you craft the stewardship message to reach parishioners with varying beliefs?

In many mainline traditions, the operating budget and the emphasis on paying bills may have been the centerpiece of the annual pledge drive for many years. Thus, congregants have been conditioned to give to the maintenance of the church—the lowest category of givers identified above. Giving to the church to help others or to strengthen their relationship with God might be new ideas, which members may or may not embrace. My experience is that a certain percentage of congregants will resist the notion that they should give to the church to help others. They can give directly to homeless shelters, disaster relief, or any other cause and do not want the church to make this decision for them.

Similarly, mainline churches may also need to demonstrate how increased giving will strengthen one's faith or relationship to God. This discussion will vary from congregation to congregation. Many parishioners believe that if the church's doors remain open, there is no reason to increase giving. They give to the operating budget rather than thinking and praying about the rewards and benefits of a growing faith.

Is Increased Giving Possible?

Sharon Miller, coeditor of *Financing American Religion*, writes in "The Meaning of Religious Giving" in that book about the chances for increased giving, She identifies "the importance of the rituals, content, and practices of worship services and other congregational events in which teachings about giving money are embedded."[11]

Mark Chaves, coeditor of the book, emphasizes Miller's point in his own article:

> Significant change in giving patterns is likely only via institutional change, by which I mean reconfiguring religious and ritual practices so that giving has a different place and meaning than it did before. Saying to a religious organization, "institutionalize a pledge system" or "train people to tithe" may be tantamount to saying "change your religious tradition." There appears to be no way to make Lutheran or Presbyterian per capita giving rise to the level of Mormon or Seventh-day Adventist giving without making Presbyterian and Lutheran religious traditions into something other than they currently are.[12]

The giving culture in your congregation and denomination may have been formulated over many decades—or perhaps centuries. If low- or same-level giving is the norm, this culture will not yield easily to change. Volunteers who lead pledge drives for a year or two in their congregations may not be able to put a substantial dent in the giving culture. Their work, however, may play an important role in beginning to change attitudes toward stewardship and the use of money among members of their congregations.

One prominent stewardship consultant will not take a contract with a congregation for less than a five-year period. He believes this to be the minimum amount of time necessary to change the giving culture in a congregation. Having led the pledge drive in my own church for two years, I can attest to the time it takes to address the range of issues presented in this book.

People who raise money are eternal optimists. They believe the money is always out there and that the more people give, the better off they will be. But it is also good to know what the worst-case scenario might be. Lay leaders will encounter some real difficulties in leading the pledge drive— low-level giving, entrenched habits, and negative attitudes toward stewardship programs and those who lead them.

While these are daunting challenges, finding and getting to know a few lionhearted donors outweigh the obstacles lay leaders are likely to encounter. Plus, we have a few surprises in store for those charitably impaired souls in your congregation!

CHAPTER 4

What Can Churches Ask Parishioners to Give?

Recently the minister of a church in a neighboring town called and said, "We're having an orientation program for new and prospective members. Could you come and provide us a glimpse into stewardship beyond our local congregation?" Since I always like to talk about creating congregations of generous people, I accepted. This church was of a denomination different from my own, and I was curious about their expectations in regard to membership and giving. What does this church ask newcomers to do? What does it ask them to give?

I went to the meeting expecting to hear church leaders talk about what the congregation was like, who they were, and the work that God called them to do. I thought the conversation would be about how church members worked and worshipped together, how they supported one another as fellow congregants, and how they engaged the larger world. I wanted to know how they grew in faith and strengthened their relationship with God from year to year.

Instead, I found what I call the "cafeteria" approach to religion. Representatives from the congregation spoke about what the church offered— men's groups, women's groups, recitals and other musical events, continuing-education programs, and various forums. There was mention of the perennial need for Sunday-school teachers, but the emphasis was on programs and events that newcomers could attend. Sunday worship was not mentioned as one of the offerings!

I was surprised at the events of this gathering because the minister in that church often railed against what he called "consumer-oriented religion." He frequently spoke of the need for parishioners to contribute their time, talent, and treasure for the betterment of the church and the larger society. Yet in his own congregation, here was an attitude of "How can we inform you, entertain you, and meet your consumer needs?" rather than one of how people work together to make God's presence more visible in their lives and in the larger world.

In their excellent book *Behind the Stained Glass Windows: Money Dynamics in the Church,* John and Sylvia Ronsvalle, researchers and writers on church giving trends, devote a lengthy section to this issue. One of their important conclusions: "Church members have changed from stewards into consumers. People are not returning a portion of their incomes to God. Rather, they are paying for services rendered by the church."[1]

My intention is not to criticize groups within congregations that meet to share personal concerns, to offer mutual support, and to pray and meditate. An important role of faith communities is to provide comfort and hope to those who struggle with significant life issues. However, it is all too easy for congregations to become passive and inward-looking, writes psychologist and pastor Robert Randall in his book *What People Expect from Church.* Randall warns that a congregation can all too easily "cultivate a climate of self-absorption, and become a consumer of its own life rather than a contributor to God's wider world."[2]

When I asked the assembled group at the orientation meeting about giving expectations, one new member replied, "There weren't any. We were told to decide on our own what to give." After the meeting I spoke with the chairman of the stewardship committee, who told me that the amount of money raised each year was about the same, even though the church had grown steadily in membership. In this congregation, new members were giving very little.

Expectations of New Members

In many congregations, the belief persists that new members, regardless of income or capacity to give, begin their membership by making small gifts or pledges. Church leaders with whom I have spoken also tend to believe that new members will be offended if the church asks them to do much or to give much. These self-defeating attitudes become self-fulfilling prophecies. Newcomers will indeed do little and give little if these are the expectations, reflecting the congregational culture.

Thus, the expectations of involvement and giving at the entry point— when people become interested in the church, when they perceive that the congregation might be a religious home for them, and when they join—can have a significant impact on giving in the congregation as a whole. If the church permits and inadvertently encourages low-level giving among new members, it is unrealistic to believe that pledge-drive leaders will elevate these expectations later. Alice Mann, a church consultant, said to me about this subject, "Low expectations among new members can even create a bait-and-switch attitude—people who were asked to give little upon joining discover to their dismay later on that the pledge drive may have significantly higher expectations."

When low-level giving becomes the norm, pledge-drive leaders sometimes believe *they* are the ones who have fallen short in trying to persuade new members (and other low-level givers) to increase their giving. New members, having received little or no guidance from the church about how charitable giving can help them create a stronger relationship with God, feel they are being harangued to give money.

The most negative description I have found of people's views toward stewardship comes from Douglas John Hall. He writes, "Stewardship has a very distasteful connotation for the majority of church folk, including clergy. It brings to mind the horror of home visitations, building projects, financial campaigns, and the seemingly incessant harping of churches for more money."[3] Stewardship volunteers need to know that negative attitudes can be common among old and new members of their congregations. Volunteers should also understand that the way they conduct stewardship initiatives can have long-lasting effects on members of the church, creating both positive and negative attitudes.

In thinking of my own experience in leading the pledge drive, I wish I had worked more closely with my congregation's membership committee. We very much needed to clarify the message our congregation communicated to new members—both expectations of church membership and charitable giving. Newcomers are more amenable to new ideas and views when they join than at any other time. Congregations should capitalize on newcomers' interest and enthusiasm! This dictum is particularly true in influencing attitudes toward stewardship. Setting higher expectations for involvement and a positive attitude toward giving among newcomers helps ensure that members are more committed to the church initially, and that they will support the church with their time and money in the months and years to come.

However, mainline congregations have a difficult time setting expectations for new members. The rector of an Episcopal congregation said, "The entry process is under scrutiny; it is something we don't do very well."

(This congregation does, however, have an excellent record of giving through special appeals, and a strong mission orientation.)

A Presbyterian minister at a nearby congregation said, "Our church needs to work on this," in response to the question about expectations of new members. And a United Methodist minister once told me authoritatively, "Nobody does membership very well."

I thought that surely some churches "did membership" well, and kept calling clergy until I reached a minister in the American Baptist Churches in the U.S.A. She had no qualms about stating her church's membership requirements. "I preach and teach tithing," she said. "As pastor I am responsible for people spiritually, and believe the biblical basis for tithing is a way of worshipping, a delight, and that people who do not tithe are missing out. I'm excited about giving."

She also sent me a page from the congregation's constitution about what constitutes membership. It lists six criteria:

- Worship regularly—at least once a week.
- Meet God daily in a set time of prayer.
- Participate in the educational program of the church.
- Engage in individual study regularly, for improvement of the mind, for enlargement of Christian experience, and in preparation of Christian service.
- Serve regularly in the programs of this church and in the areas of Christian responsibility outside of this church.
- Dedicate a tithe of income to the work of the Kingdom of God.[4]

There are no doubts about membership expectations in this church! Yet with the exception of the tithe, these criteria could apply to many traditions. I believe mainline congregations could benefit from a greater understanding of why people in high-expectation traditions give so much to their churches. My experience has been that mainline congregations do not subscribe to the conservative theologies of high-expectation churches, and thus believe there is little to be learned from them. "Mainliners" could learn a great deal from high-expectation groups, in particular how they instill a significant degree of commitment, service, and generosity. Members of mainline churches would also benefit from learning where they stand in membership and giving requirements relative to American churchgoers in general.

People who belong to high-expectation churches believe that God has given them everything they have. Not only that—God lets them keep 90 percent of it. What a deal! They are enriched by the experience of giving. Keeping a large share of God's blessings stands in stark contrast to the attitude in many mainline congregations—that charitable giving implies having to give up something; and thus we may be worse off than before.

In high-expectation traditions, giving 10 percent of one's income is expected of church members regardless of income level, and applies to rich and poor alike. (I recall hearing that a church member once said he made too much money to tithe!) In some traditions, tithing is the *minimum* expectation, usually for the ongoing support of the church. Giving to campaigns for new construction, renovation, or missions is sought in addition to the tithe. For example, many Mormon congregations collect what are called "fast offerings." On the first Sunday of each month, parishioners are asked to fast for two meals and to donate to the church the amount that would have been spent on these meals. These funds are held by the local bishop in a discretionary fund, to be allocated to church members in financial need.

Many traditions also encourage members to increase the percentage of their gift-giving as they grow in faith. While not everyone in these churches tithes, some give much more than 10 percent, even as much as 25 percent to 50 percent of their incomes.

Some high-expectation churches also encourage members to make sacrifices to meet their giving obligations. In the Assemblies of God, members are encouraged to buy less expensive houses and cars, to forgo the purchase of furniture and appliances, to take less costly vacations, to get their hair cut less often, and to eat in restaurants less frequently—all so they can increase their giving to God.

Many African-American churches also maintain a tradition of multiple collections during the Sunday service. In *The Good Book*, Peter Gomes, minister of Memorial Church at Harvard University, writes,

> White people who visit black churches are often surprised and not
> a little shocked at the number of offerings given, and with the fine
> art of encouraging people to generosity. It takes them some time
> to realize that the giving of money is not a necessary condition to
> the material needs of the people of God, but rather it is the central
> drama in the act of worship.[5]

Gomes also writes about observing the offering when he was a young child. The plate was not passed in the pews; instead people would bring their gifts forward to the front of the church. There was a dollar goal to be met each Sunday, and the stewards would count the money as it was given. If the goal was not met on the first go-around, the choir would continue singing and the congregation was asked to pass up front again, until the goal was reached.

"It was high theater for a child," Gomes writes, "with the whole congregation on view and in motion, the murmuring of the stewards as they counted, the relentless rhythm of the singing, and the anxious moments while awaiting the result."[6]

Ministers and lay leaders in mainline denominations might look with bewilderment and some envy at churches whose members give so generously and joyfully. Yet in their heart of hearts, they may feel themselves and their fellow parishioners incapable of ever giving so much.

Perhaps the ultimate example of high expectations and sharing with God is set by a small Mennonite congregation in Indiana. Each year in the late spring, church members gather and share their federal 1040 income-tax forms with one another, so that all will know they have returned the appropriate portion to God.

These examples of high-expectation giving are ones that members of your mainline congregation would probably never consider, and may in fact find preposterous. Yet, these examples should be a part of stewardship in your congregation. Most mainline congregations consist of solidly middle-class households that give about 1.7 percent of income to the church or to other causes. This percentage is considerably less than that given by members of high-expectation churches. I believe the examples of charitable giving set by high-expectation traditions are extraordinarily inspiring because they include people from lower economic groups. Not only are they uplifting, but also in my experience, using these examples will reduce the number of complaints from middle-class members about the church asking for too much money.

These examples raise the question of how much a church can ask from its parishioners. One more story, and then let's look at an answer or two.

Charles Bennison, Episcopal bishop of Pennsylvania, was earlier in his career the rector of St. Mark's Episcopal Church, Upland, California. Of this church he said, "In the early 1980s, our church had 700 members, but stewardship was a great frustration. We had been on a plateau for nine years. The newest members got stuck with the pledge drive and had little support. We tried kickoff dinners and events, home visits, different letters. Nothing worked very well."

"One day," Bennison continued, "a well-respected woman in the congregation invited me to lunch. During our conversation, she asked if I tithed to the church. At the time I did not. She said if I tithed, she would take over the stewardship program and run it more successfully than I had ever imagined possible."

Bennison and his wife prayed about the decision they were asked to make, and agreed to tithe. In a subsequent board retreat, the woman (who tithed also) persuaded vestry members to tithe, or to put in place a plan to tithe. "That decision was not made easily," Bennison recalled, "but we did it. One member ranted and raved, saying that if he had intended to tithe, he would have become a Mormon. The congregation's reaction and the jolt of new money revolutionized the church. Within two years, our parish led the Los Angeles Diocese in per-capita giving. We also raised money for a new building [and] a new school, and purchased two apartment buildings that were used for transitional housing."

"A great deal of what we accomplished," Bennison concluded, "was to define what the church stood for, and what we were committed to. We created high standards in this parish, and newcomers did what others were doing. A ripple effect is that we were able to turn people into true leaders."

What Churches Can Ask

So what can your churches ask members to give? Here are a few things to keep in mind while coming up with an answer:

1. In most congregations, the majority of annual gifts fall within the $200-to-$1,600 range, about $16 to $135 per month, or $4 to $30 per week. Most members of mainline Protestant traditions could probably double their pledges and hardly notice the difference in their checkbooks. Few churches, however, would dare to ask for this much.

If you intend to ask parishioners to increase their giving, be prepared for some people to inform you that no one could possibly give what you're asking. This kind of comment usually means that your informant will not give more. In many churches, even in the most affluent areas, the perception abides that parishioners cannot give more even if they live in expensive homes, drive late-model cars, take lavish vacations, and enroll their children in expensive private schools. (Or they can't give to the church because they've spent all their money on these things.)

2. In many churches, parishioners will not give more than the minister and members of the governing body are giving. Even if parishioners don't know what the minister or board members give, they have an uncanny sixth sense about not being too far out in front of anyone else, especially the leadership.

This finding means that the cumulative amount that the minister(s) and governing body pledge to the church should be communicated to the congregation. The example they set is a critical factor in the success of the pledge drive.

3. In considering how much to ask parishioners to give, some churches use formulas. Some Unitarian Universalist congregations, for example, have been asking parishioners who pledge above $1,000 per year to give 10 percent more, and those below $1,000 per year to add $100. (This approach asks higher donors to increase their giving by a lower percentage, and smaller donors by a higher percentage.) Another approach favored by those who use weekly envelopes is asking everyone for a certain dollar-per-week increase. Yet other churches provide financial worksheets on which parishioners calculate an appropriate gift by taking into account gross household income, mortgage payments, utilities, college tuition, and other fixed expenses.

Some congregations find that these formulas work because they offer parishioners guidelines for giving. If clergy and lay leaders hear the comment, "People don't know how much they should give," they face a serious issue, one that reflects poor communication about stewardship in the congregation. However, if members really don't know how much to give and are seeking recommendations, you have been provided an excellent opportunity to introduce higher-level giving!

Many stewardship leaders with whom I have spoken claim that formulas are successful. I believe they are because they ask people for so little, often beginning at 1 percent of income. I also believe that formulas are not equitable. For example, asking everyone for a five-dollar weekly increase might mean a sacrifice for a single parent, but would be a pittance for a wealthy family. A slight increase achieved by formula giving may provide for this church year, but formulas can also impose ceilings beyond which many parishioners will not go. Also, as we discussed in the previous chapter, 80 percent of parishioners may not respond to calls for increased giving, whatever formula is used. In my view, formulas do not address the issue of generosity in our lives, which should be the ultimate goal.

If formulas have been successful in your congregation, so much the better. If you wish to increase giving in your congregation by using a formula, you might increase the percentage that people are asked to give. Believe it or not, many people might not notice, or might accept the new percentage as part of the general inflationary economic trend. The approaches to increased giving that I describe in this book are not intended to represent a single way to conduct stewardship programs. You can introduce any number of methods, including formulas.

The Answer to the Question

We can now answer the question of how much money churches can ask people to give. If you believe that a growing faith in God and our lives are made better through what we share, then the answer to how much churches and synagogues can ask members to give is clear:

Charitable giving should make some difference in how we as religious people experience life from day to day. If giving to your congregation is similar to writing a check at the end of the month to pay the phone bill or the electric bill, and then forgetting about it until the end of the next month, you are not giving enough.

Similarly, if you take spare change or a dollar or two from your pocket or purse for the weekly collection and never notice the difference, your giving has too little meaning either for you or for your church.

Silvio Nardoni, treasurer for the Pacific Southwest District of the Unitarian Universalist Association, has emphasized this point: "Charitable giving should change your life in some way." This is the standard of giving for all individuals and households.

Of course, the amount that people can give will vary from household to household. The way that volunteers conduct stewardship initiatives in your congregation should reinforce parishioners' belief that they are doing the right thing. Charles Jaffee, a noted financial columnist, once wrote, "Increase your charitable giving. Doing the right thing is more important than money; it will make you feel as good or better than hitting all the rest of your financial targets."[7]

Charitable giving helps people live righteous lives. Being religious people and sharing in good measure should change our lives—forever. This is your goal.

CHAPTER 5

The Budget Isn't Really
That Important

Church treasurers might wince at the title of this chapter. After all, salaries and benefits must be paid. The building requires heat and lighting, insurance, cleaning, and maintenance. The Sunday school needs juice and crackers. Everyone knows it costs money to run churches from day to day.

The intent of this chapter is not to lessen the role of the treasurer, the work of the finance committee, or the need for an effective budget process. There is no doubt about the value of the budget, the necessity of accurate figures, and the legal requirements of adhering to accepted accounting principles.

The operating budget is not important, however, in regard to how the pledge drive is conducted. Consultant and author Ashley Hale writes, "Almost all budgets are compromised, watered-down documents. The average budget provides no reason for generous giving and countless excuses for token giving. It is at best hesitant and fearful and at worst static and apologetic."[1]

I agree with Hale. In most congregations, clergy and lay leaders make cautious financial decisions. Expenditures are modest. Costs are kept in check. New ways to spend money are viewed with suspicion. Many congregations routinely operate on the tradition of "just enough money to scrape by and no more." To use a retail analogy, I believe churches return far more in value than members pay for. Church is one of the great bargains of all time, and the typical budget process ensures that this will remain the case in the future.

Many congregations use the budget as the centerpiece of the pledge drive out of habit and not because the practice is effective. As a result, pledge drives focus on incremental increases over the previous year. Insurance will cost $90 more. Dues to the denomination are increasing $3 per member. Other small costs creep in. Thus, running the church will cost 2 percent more than last year. These inconsequential increases create the belief that parishioners can give the same or only a few dollars more—just enough to cover costs. The church pays its bills and will endure for time eternal.

During the economic boom of the 1990s, income rose for 90 percent of American households, yet charitable giving to churches per capita decreased. I believe the traditional budget process, with its emphasis on negligible increases and paying the bills, has inadvertently created and perpetuated low-level and same-level giving among church members.

The conventional wisdom is that parishioners want to know how their money will be spent before they make pledges or gifts; that is, they want to see the budget. That is a myth. People want to know that their money will not be spent foolishly. But unless the church has a history of financial impropriety, few parishioners take more than a fleeting interest in the annual operating budget.

For example, as a consultant I recommended to church leaders in a growing congregation that they not include the budget in the annual pledge publication, as had been the custom. Instead, a sidebar paragraph stated that copies of the budget were available in the church office. Anyone could stop by and pick one up. Not a single person requested the budget. This congregation of about 450 members passed the budget unanimously at the annual meeting a few months later with only minor questions from members.

The Pledge Drive Should Come Before the Budget

In many congregations the operating budget is formulated by the treasurer or finance committee, then forwarded to the pledge committee. The budget figures are presented to the congregation as an integral part of the annual pledge drive. If this is the case in your congregation, you need to reverse the order!

Regardless of a church's fiscal year or whether the congregation conducts its pledge drive in fall or spring, the pledge drive should always come before the budget is formulated. Giving to a budget is not inspiring. Giving to the budget defeats the whole idea of generosity as a fundamental religious principle, of returning to God some proportion of what we have been given, and building a stronger faith. It doesn't matter what the operating budget is. In fact, a congregation that gives more to the church might break out of that hesitant, fearful, apologetic tradition, as Ashley Hale suggests, that budgets impose on congregations.

Why the Budget Is So Uninteresting to So Many

Let's take a brief look at how the budget is formulated to see why so few people are interested in it. The budget process often covers a period of weeks or months, usually beginning with the treasurer's requesting estimated costs for the coming year from each committee chair. How much will the church spend for salaries, benefits, denominational dues, religious education, mission and outreach, Sunday-school materials, snow removal, air conditioning, and dozens of other items?

Many people don't like dealing with budgets—at home, at work, or at church. Committee chairs often view preparing budget figures as a slightly disagreeable chore. Lay leaders who don't know how much to ask for are often told, "Just base your request on last year's figure." Some committee chairs, including a few of the old-timers, don't respond to requests for budget figures at all because they know the board will allocate about the same amount as the previous year anyway. In addition, since most church budgets are tight, with little extra money, a zero-sum game goes into effect—spending more in one area would require taking it from another. Most committee chairs will not risk a confrontation by asking for more money, which would mean budgeting less for another area of ministry.

In addition, since this year's pledge drive is expected to raise the same amount as last year's, the budget process relegates committees to doing about what they did the previous year. The eventual result of the traditional budget process is that committees will get the same amount of money from year to year, give or take a little.

In his book *The Middle-Sized Church* Lyle Schaller writes about this practice from a slightly different point of view. He suggests that "many churches tend to recreate yesterday."[2] The thinking is that if last year in the church was OK, then why change anything? Many parishioners enjoy the familiarity and predictability of church life. If parishioners move away, then visit the church years later, they hope everything will be the same as they remembered it, as though nothing had changed in the intervening time.

Tradition is important for the liturgical calendar. The fall, winter, and spring seasons bring predictable and meaningful holy days and holidays.

But tradition and familiar habits can too easily become institutionalized, providing mainly for the comfort and convenience of current members. Familiar patterns do not challenge congregations to dream larger dreams or reach out to address society's problems. Schaller notes somewhat caustically that "some churches think next year is 1957, and plan accordingly."[3]

It is important to note that small churches view the budget in a different light from large churches. Anthony Pappas, in his book *Money, Motivation, and Mission in the Small Church*, notes a lack of understanding in stewardship literature about small churches increasing their budgets so that they can always do more. He writes, "No small church of which I am aware responds to well-doing. People in small churches are already doing more. They feel a sense of responsibility that, in all honesty, can itself be tiring! The call to give more to do more is akin to attempting to persuade a Bedouin to buy a truckload of sand."[4]

All too often, the budget process focuses on the familiar and reinforces our inclination to recreate yesterday. Even if congregational leaders recognize that additional time, effort, and money should go into a new or important initiative, it is difficult to get a committee to spend a larger sum unless strong leadership presses for it. I am familiar with committees in more than one congregation that were offered additional funds and literally did not know what to do with the money.

I recall attending the annual meeting of a large congregation in an affluent suburban community during which an elderly woman stood and said she had come into some extra money. She would consider a $10,000 gift if someone could tell her what the church would do with it. The music director immediately said, "More music," provoking laughter from the congregation. But neither the minister nor the church leadership had anything else to add. The woman stood silently for a few moments, then took her seat. To my knowledge, she did not make the gift to the church.

Church treasurers and those interested in financial matters eventually realize that few people care about the budget. Some treasurers actually prefer this inattention, because they don't get questions about church spending from parishioners who are uninformed about how budgets work.

Not only are most parishioners uninterested in the budget, but many find financial matters in church a nuisance. They often buy items for the church out of their own pockets rather than complete the paperwork to get cash in advance. They don't save receipts and fill out reimbursement forms unless the items they buy are expensive. Even though parishioners may have been encouraged countless times not to buy things out of their own funds so that the church can keep an accurate accounting of costs, they are likely to persist in doing so. (I have to confess that I do this myself.) So in many congregations, there is also a "stealth budget," money spent by parishioners that isn't accounted for on the books.

The majority of parishioners give the budget only a passing glance. They will be curious about the minister's salary, if it is listed. Or, they might look for any significant increases over last year in certain line items. But most parishioners trust church leaders to make prudent financial decisions.

The colorful pie charts so easily compiled using computer spreadsheets and color printers give parishioners an accurate indication of how money is raised and spent in the church. While helpful, charts and graphs reinforce the notion that the pie has a standard size. A larger slice here means a smaller slice there. Your job is to introduce the idea that the pie itself can be infinitely larger, and so can all of its pieces. Don't let your pledge drive be driven by budget figures and minuscule line-item increases.

Budget figures should be part of the information shared about how money is raised and spent in the congregation. But keep in mind that numbers are boring to many, misunderstood by others, and uninspiring to just about everyone—not ingredients for a successful pledge drive!

Inspirational Giving

Think about the last time you received a solicitation for a charitable gift. Most likely it was a letter from your alma mater, a local hospital, theater group, youth sports team, symphony orchestra, museum, or social-service agency. The letter probably informed you of what the organization was doing, that the previous year was one of the best, that next year would be even better, and that wonderful things would happen if you sent in a check.

For instance, your gift would help the college provide scholarships to needy students. The symphony would perform a world premiere. The hospital would make great strides in treating a particular disease. The theater group would stage a work written by a local playwright. A homeless shelter would provide people with basic needs. The youth sports team would build character in the younger generation.

All these organizations appealed to your heart and soul. Your gift would help them achieve wonderful things. You would be a meaningful part of a meaningful cause. In much the same way that people vote for political candidates, they make charitable gifts for emotional and not necessarily rational reasons.

Secular organizations that raise money also attempt to instill trust in donors and confidence that money won't be spent carelessly. These organizations also ask for increased financial support year after year, as they attempt to reach new heights. The dollar goal never decreases. An implicit understanding prevails that running a school or museum obviously costs more with each passing year. The more you give, the greater the organization, the greater your personal fulfillment. Their banners do not read, "Give to us, so we can do about the same as last year."

Churches should take note. Parishioners have powerful emotional attachments to their churches. They give to the church because they or their parents were married in the building. Perhaps a memorial service for a loved one was conducted there. Maybe they have memories of their infants being baptized, their children singing in a choir for the first time, or their teenagers being part of a youth group. Maybe they recall the church reaching out and helping a friend or relative in need. They give because this building is where they worship, where they express their faith in God.

These powerful emotions motivate people to give to churches or synagogues. Charitable giving in a religious context is not merely a financial matter. It is an emotional and spiritual commitment that helps define our relationship with God over the course of our lives. Sharing what we have is how we accomplish what God calls us to do in this time and place. On the newsstands and on television these days, we are told that growing numbers of people both in and out of churches find the secular life wanting and are seeking deeper spiritual commitment and involvement. It is just not good enough for churches to be complacent, for each church year to repeat the one just past, to provide parishioners and potential newcomers with lukewarm opportunities that do not stir their hearts and souls.

Author Ashley Hale writes, "Let's replace the dreary, lockstep annual budget with a thoughtfully prepared list of what the church could do and even what it should do. The issue is not whether the church will survive, but whether it will flourish."[5]

Will members of your congregation flourish? I visited a church recently and talked with members of the congregation about the budget process and the other issues described above. Following my remarks a woman said to me, "I've been in this congregation for eight years, and don't believe I have grown in spirit or in faith since I joined." This was a sad statement. The church struck me as an interesting place, and the members seemed thoughtful. Yet in talking with parishioners I discerned an element of "sameness" about church life from year to year. Many factors beyond the budget process no doubt contributed to this malaise. Members of the congregation were not unhappy with the church but seemed resigned to its current state of affairs. The church was what it was. Members wanted their church to be a more important part of their lives, but they didn't know how to make it happen.

I felt that if all members of this congregation doubled or tripled their pledges, it would signal a renewed life—for the congregation as a whole, and for the pride and satisfaction that individuals would gain in seeing what their congregation could accomplish. Don't allow the budget process to stifle the hopes and dreams of your congregation and your attempts to implement more effective stewardship initiatives.

In 1929 theologian H. Richard Niebuhr wrote, "American religion is not the religion of that middle class which struggled with kings and popes in the defense of its economic and religious liberties but the religion of a bourgeoisie whose conflicts are over and which has passed into the quiet waters of assured income and established social standing."[6]

I believe the religious spirit remains strong among American churchgoers of all ages today. But the tentative and cautious ways of many churches have created those quiet waters that Niebuhr wrote about 70 years ago. Attempts to create a congregation of generous people should stir up those still waters and create a mighty flowing stream!

CHAPTER 6

The Minister's Role in Fund-Raising

Before Diane Miller was called to First Parish, a 140-year-old church in a suburban area, the congregation conducted a survey of its membership. The survey included questions about parishioners' ages, length of membership, number of children, attendance at worship, and other general information. One section pertained to the minister's duties. These included preaching, religious education, and pastoral care. Congregants were asked to rank in importance some 12 items, including fund-raising.

Ranking last among the members' expectations of the minister was fund-raising. The minister was expected to play no role in raising money beyond preaching an annual stewardship sermon. Many ministers would feel a sense of relief at finding a church with such low expectations for their involvement in fund-raising. It is unrealistic, however, for ministers and lay leaders alike to believe that the minister can be removed entirely from fund-raising and other financial issues in the parish.

Frances Harris, treasurer at First Parish, did not agree with the survey results. She said, "If ministers aren't involved in financial matters, it sends the message that money is not an appropriate subject to address in church. It can also be interpreted as the minister abdicating responsibility for a vital part of church life, leaving it for others to deal with."

The discussion in this chapter focuses on congregations with a solo minister. In multi-staff congregations, an associate or assistant minister might assume stewardship responsibilities rather than the senior minister. Such an arrangement is perfectly acceptable.

The minister needs to take a well-thought-out and meaningful role in stewardship education. However, the minister's role will vary from congregation to congregation. Many ministers are uncomfortable asking for money. Some clergy believe it is inappropriate to call for increased giving, as their salaries are usually one of the largest items in the church budget and closely tied to the annual pledge drive. Loren Mead, an Episcopal priest, once wrote, "I was asking people to pledge to God, but I knew the money was coming to me."[1]

Mead also writes about other issues involving clergy and money, of which laypeople are usually unaware. These include the belief that inadequate salaries are virtuous; the concern that clergy are not paid in proportion to the education and training required for successful ministry; feelings of resentment toward parishioners of means who contribute little to the church; and feelings of economic inferiority (for example, when congregants want to pass along leftover furniture and clothing.)[2] Clearly, there are complex issues surrounding clergy and money, and the appropriate role of the minister. Lay leaders should recognize and respect the minister's feelings toward money in the congregation.

In his book *The Steward* Douglas John Hall may reflect a common attitude among clergy toward raising money in the congregation. He writes, "Ministers cringe at the mention of stewardship Sundays: must they lower themselves to the status of fund-raisers once more?"[3] A few ministers with whom I have spoken view fund-raising as an unpleasant aspect of their work. One minister said he believed fund-raising to be the antithesis of religious leadership.

Other clergy, however, feel no hesitation whatever about discussing money in church. They believe money is the means to accomplish God's work, and the more people give, the more their religious values are expressed. The late Cardinal Richard Cushing, a Catholic leader noted for his extraordinary ability to raise money and build new churches, is rumored to have said, "When I was a young man, I couldn't decide whether to go into religion or into business. I'm always glad I chose business." Some ministers have the gift. Most do not.

In his essay "Clergy as Reluctant Stewards," in *Financing American Religion*, Daniel Conway, director of stewardship and development for the Roman Catholic Archdiocese of Chicago, summarizes the results of a survey of clergy attitudes toward training for the ministry. A sizable majority of respondents indicated that they were satisfied or extremely satisfied with their education in theological and pastoral subjects. However, less than 15 percent were satisfied with the administrative or financial training they had received.[4]

Conway also noted that while clergy often take continuing-education courses throughout their careers, the courses that held the least interest were related to church finance. Thus, while clergy are dissatisfied with their training in financial matters, Conway writes, "Paradoxically, they appear uninterested in continuing education courses that might help them become better stewards of their congregation's human, physical, and financial resources."[5]

A number of ministers with whom I have spoken do not perceive that they would gain additional benefits through continuing education in finance or administration, as they do not view these as core elements of ministry. Other aspects of ministry that affect parishioners' lives are seen as more critical. One minister told me she was interested in learning about financial issues, adding that the training would be more beneficial if lay leaders accompanied her, so they could learn to work together as a team in managing church finances.

A friend of mine is a layperson in a church that recently undertook what was called "the legacy process." The legacy committee examined what the congregation was doing today to determine what legacy current church members would leave to their children and to future generations. Among the issues examined was the role of the minister. Members of the congregation knew that his strengths were preaching and pastoral care, not finance and administration. This is the case in many congregations. But members of this congregation took a fresh look at the role that lay leaders needed to play, particularly in church finance. The minister would be an integral part of all financial decisions, but his daily responsibilities in managing the church's financial affairs would be assumed by lay leaders.

The division of duties into pastoral and financial segments appears to be a common model. Anthony Kill, a minister in the United Church of Christ, described his role in this way: "I take an active part in planning and monitoring the church's finances," he said, "but I am not involved in the day-to-day management of financial affairs. This is carried out by lay leaders. My main role is to create the vision to grow, which in turn creates financial strength. When I preach a stewardship sermon, sometimes the topic is money, but sometimes it is vision."

The minister's role in stewardship should be examined on a case-by-case basis. A good rule: Play to the minister's strengths. This is a good rule for laypeople as well. For example, some clergy and lay members are excellent speakers and can deliver stirring sermons or addresses. Others may be exceptional writers and can craft compelling letters, pamphlets, brochures, or other communications. Some people may be artistic and can design eye-catching print materials (or Web sites). Yet others may be out-going and hospitable, able to meet people easily, and speak enthusiastically about the work of the church. Some people may have been involved in capital campaigns for their colleges or other nonprofit agencies and enjoy the excitement of asking for charitable gifts face to face. A stewardship leader needs to ascertain what people are comfortable doing, and support them in their various roles. This guideline includes the minister, who should be viewed in a positive context by the congregation in whatever role he or she eventually plays.

What All Ministers Should Be Able to Do

The minister plays a critical role in promoting stewardship in five ways:

1. *The minister should introduce the importance of stewardship to the congregation at the earliest opportunity.* This task is most effec-tively accomplished by the minister's making a leadership gift to the church. Most people in the congregation know the minister's salary and the level of commitment he or she has made. Parishioners' own giving may or may not be influenced by the minister's gift. It is a mistake, in fact, for the minister to believe that if he or she makes a sizable pledge, others will automatically follow that example. But the minister's role in the congregation and his or her credibility is significantly enhanced by a generous annual gift.

In some traditions, ministers are appointed to churches. In others, a search is conducted in the same way a nonprofit organization seeks an executive director or a college selects a faculty member. Whichever method is used, I believe the minister should state his or her giving intentions before accepting the call or appointment to a congregation. This statement helps es-tablish the minister's credibility and gives notice to the congregation that steward-ship will be an important element of church life—literally from day one.

I believe that ministers who contribute generously to their congrega-tions enjoy greater respect and are less prone to criticism from parishio-ners—especially low-level donors and nondonors, who in many congrega-tions are the most cantankerous. In my experience, parishioners who give the most are those who ask the least in return. Conversely, parishioners who give the least complain most frequently, and are usually the least will-ing to work toward changing the situation they are unhappy about.

Last, in regard to the minister's gift to the church, if the time arrives for the minister to become involved in asking for a significant gift from a parishioner, he or she does so from a position of respect, authority, and credibility. I believe generosity begets generosity. Clergy who are generous to their congregations will find that their congregations are generous in return—sometimes in direct financial ways, such as forgiving a loan or mortgage; or in personal ways, in the respect and many kindnesses the congregation displays toward its minister on a regular basis. Generous clergy are rewarded in many ways.

2. *The minister should stress the importance of ongoing stewardship education with new or incoming members.* This is a role that stewardship volunteers *must* supplement. As we discussed in the previous chapter, lay leaders should work closely with the minister and the membership committee in defining acceptable giving standards for new and incoming members. The minister should be an integral part of these discussions, as new members will look to him or her for guidance, even if giving expectations are conveyed by lay leaders.

A widespread belief prevails that new members begin pledging low amounts and only increase their giving as they become more involved in the church. In some instances, this pattern may hold sway. But in others, it may be that low-pledging newcomers will take their places among the 80 percent of congregants who cannot articulate why they give what they give, and who become resistant to increasing their giving to the church.

I believe the standard for giving among newcomers should assume that charitable giving will make a difference in one's life. This is the same standard for all members of the congregation, old or new. Newcomers to the congregation should also be asked to make a financial commitment when they join—not whenever the next pledge drive rolls around.

3. *The minister should encourage an attitude of abundance rather than scarcity.* Giving is the nature of God. In giving to the church, we give to strengthen our own congregations, to help the less fortunate, and to deepen our relationship to God. Churches should not take an apologetic attitude toward asking people to give but should encourage generosity from members at all income levels. (Keep in mind that high-expectation churches expect the tithe from all members, regardless of income.) Churches should provide members with frequent giving opportunities, so that the practice of giving becomes part of the life of the congregation. Giving should become second nature to people in the congregation. Look for outgoing people who will speak frequently, enthusiastically, and publicly throughout the year about how wonderful these giving opportunities are!

In creating an atmosphere of generosity, keep in mind that churches are not the protector of peoples' wallets, pocketbooks, or bank accounts. People can decide whether they wish to give or not, and parishioners will not give more than they can afford. Most congregations encourage people to make weekly offerings on Sunday mornings, reinforcing the habit of regular giving as a part of worship. Others provide parishioners only a few opportunities to give—the annual pledge paid out monthly or quarterly, or even in a single payment, and maybe a Christmas and Easter plate offering. If your congregation offers only a few giving opportunities throughout the year, you are perpetuating an element of scarcity and depriving people of ways they can live more fulfilling lives and accomplish the work of God.

If you provide your congregation numerous opportunities to give throughout the year, many congregants will respond—maybe not to every appeal, but likely to more than one. They will feel proud of what they have accomplished. If you get a few complaints from parishioners about asking for money too often, tell them about the great things that are being accomplished at church, and aren't they fortunate to be a part of it! Giving is not drudgery. The minister's relentless enthusiasm will demonstrate to parishioners that giving money away is just about the best thing they can do in life!

4. *The minister has the task of setting a vision and clarifying roles.* In the previous chapter we discussed the value of congregations having goals, a mission, or a vision. Some ministers are very clear about the mission of the church. Others are not. Be aware that members' expectations of the minister run high. Ministers are responsible for preaching, teaching, attending to pastoral duties, counseling, conducting weddings and memorial services, managing staff, and carrying out myriad other tasks—all with charm and grace. Ministers are often swept along by day-to-day church life and the relentless demands of the job; they need the aid and support of lay leaders and members of the congregation in setting and maintaining the church's larger vision.

Setting a vision may be among a minister's strengths. If not, ministers at least should articulate what they wish to accomplish while serving a congregation. Most ministers prefer to focus on preaching, teaching, and pastoral care. These functions are what attracted them to ministry in the first place. If this is the case, ministers should articulate this preference to their congregations. They should discuss how they view ministry, and the things they do well. Clarifying the minister's role will help lay leaders complement the minister's strengths in providing congregational leadership—for example, in stewardship and financial matters.

Few ministers desire to take on additional fund-raising and administrative responsibilities. The congregation could greatly assist the minister by ensuring that lay leaders are well trained in their respective roles, especially church stewardship and financial management. This preparation includes adequate orientation and training when they assume leadership roles, as well as continuing-education courses that are offered in most areas of the country by denominational programs and services.

5. *The minister makes stewardship part of the worship service on a regular basis.* Cheryl Minor, an Episcopal rector, preaches from a three-year lectionary, as do ministers of many mainline churches. Whenever money is the topic of Scripture, she preaches about it. "During the first year of my new ministry," she said, "the topic of money in Scripture came up frequently. Some parishioners said they had heard more money sermons in that first year than in many years combined! This year, there are fewer references in the lectionary, so I have discussed stewardship less." In contrast, some ministers, who may or may not preach from a lectionary, don't like to talk about money at all and rarely discuss the subject from the pulpit.

Ministers and lay leaders need to determine how often money should be discussed in their congregations. Some ministers insist that attendance at worship is lower on Stewardship Sunday when the "money sermon" is preached. An important way the minister can address low attendance is by explaining that the stewardship sermon is not a pitch for money. Rather, Stewardship Sunday is a means by which we strengthen our faith. It is a matter of lifelong learning, similar to other aspects of leading a religious life.

Discussing stewardship in a once-a-year sermon is not sufficient. On the other hand, too-frequent references to money may bring accusations that the minister talks about money too much—charges that even ministerial enthusiasm may not quell. Congregations need to find a delicate balance. One way to discuss money throughout the church year is to thank people more often. If your congregation has initiated new programs or services or has accomplished more because of a successful pledge drive, remind people that their gifts to the church made that possible. If a youth minister, assistant choir director, or education director has been added, make sure that these new staff people are visible during Sunday worship. Remind congregants of how additional staff or programs have enhanced and enriched church life. If the choir acquired new robes or the church bought a new van, congregants can be reminded that everyone derives great satisfaction from what they have accomplished together. Allow congregants to feel good about what they have done. People cannot be thanked too many times, and parishioners' appreciation for their good deeds helps build the foundation for ongoing stewardship over the months and years to come.

In his book *44 Ways to Increase the Financial Base of Your Congregation*, Lyle Schaller includes a chapter on special appeals that can be conducted throughout the church year.[6] These appeals are in addition to the annual pledge drive. I recommend this chapter highly (the book is one of the best ever written on stewardship), because it articulates interesting and appealing ways that churches can address the subject of money throughout the church year.

Robert Tobin, an Episcopal priest, provides an example of how clergy can engage a congregation in charitable giving beyond the annual pledge drive. When Hurricane Mitch devastated parts of Honduras, Tobin was moved by the suffering he saw. On the following Sunday he told the congregation how he felt and said he was going to give $1,000 for relief efforts. He invited congregants to give also. The result was $16,000 in member contributions, an amount matched by an anonymous donor. The congregation sent $32,000, along with a number of volunteers who traveled to Honduras and helped in relief efforts. The congregation received regular reports from their volunteers in Honduras and took great pride in the work they had accomplished as a religious community. This is a wonderful example of giving beyond the annual pledge drive.

A Ministerial Caveat

Ministers who take active roles in stewardship programs should realize that a number of issues call for exercising caution. For example, should they know how much parishioners give to the church? Ministers have strong feelings on this subject. Some ministers learn in seminary that the amount a person gives to the church should be known only to God (and, one assumes, to the church treasurer). A common belief among ministers is that they don't want to know what people give because they are concerned about favoritism toward those who give more, presumed to be the wealthier families.

Some arguments favor the minister's knowing what people give to the church. The most pragmatic is that some parishioners will give more because they wish to be held in high esteem by the clergy. A growing number of ministers also believe charitable giving is an integral part of a person's spiritual well-being, and seek to help parishioners in thinking and praying about this important issue. Some ministers believe the annual pledge drive is a barometer that helps measure congregational life and that variations in giving might indicate the need for a pastoral call. Some ministers also believe that knowing the amount someone gives to the church is similar to knowing their investment of time and talent, and is an important indication of what parishioners contribute to the congregation as a whole. Yet other ministers believe that congregants who are the most generous are also the best candidates for leadership roles in the church, as they are committed to the faith.

My conviction is that ministers should know how much parishioners give to the church. This knowledge allows the minister to thank those who are generous in proportion to their means. Remember, those who are charitably inclined are your angels. They are the church pillars, the leaders who support the church and (usually) the minister over the long haul, through good times and bad. They should be encouraged for their generosity and their good deeds. What purpose is served if members who deeply love the church go unacknowledged by the minister?

Should Ministers Tell How Much They Give?

"When I was a parish minister," says Loren Mead, "I told the congregation what I pledged. But the issue can be very volatile. Part of our American culture is avoiding topics like this. You need to get some benchmarks out there. If ministers think it will be helpful, they should tell parishioners. If not, its better to avoid the issue. I generally feel the more openness, the better."

Charles Kast, pastor of the Community Church in Chapel Hill, North Carolina, has done both. "When I began in ministry 18 years ago, I didn't tell anyone what I gave. About nine years into my ministry I began keeping track of how I spent my time and money. I was giving a small amount and decided to increase the percentage each year. Now I have reached 10 percent, the tithe. Along the way I decided to tell the congregation the amount of my gift. I am among the highest givers, and everyone knows my salary, so they realize how large an amount this is for me. I don't tell people this is what they should do. I just tell them how I came to my decision. I found that if I talked about money, others would, too."

Peter Luton, senior minister of the East Shore Unitarian Church in Bellevue, Washington, has gone the opposite direction. "I used to tell the congregation the amount of my pledge," he said. "At the time, I was serving a smaller congregation. I think the usefulness of my telling was that by and large the congregation was low-pledging. This new idea of how to think about one's pledge would have been better served had I been able to get other members to openly discuss their pledge commitments. I stopped talking about the amount of my pledge when I got married and didn't like putting my wife on the spot regarding our pledge to the church. I also learned that stewardship sermons should be vision-based and celebratory. Bringing up dollar amounts in sermons detracts from that larger message."

I agree with Mead that the more openness about money in church, the more likely parishioners will examine their own views of stewardship and charitable giving. But the decision as to whether ministers should tell their congregations about their own giving is an intensely personal one. Some ministers feel comfortable doing so, while others view their giving as a private matter.

Current stewardship volunteers and church workers contemplating leadership of the congregation's pledge drive need to understand clearly the minister's attitude toward money in the church. Clergy opinions vary. If the minister is a visible enthusiast, the pledge-drive leader's job will be easier because the cultural norms about money in the congregation will likely be positive. If not, volunteers will need to seek support and enthusiasm among key lay leaders.

Under no circumstances should one accept leadership of the pledge drive if enthusiasm is lacking in both minister and lay leaders. Their support is critical to effective stewardship. The other essential ingredients that stewardship volunteers need are the subject of the following chapter.

PART II

Putting a Long-Term Stewardship Program in Place

CHAPTER 7

The Essential Checklist: Important Things to Know

We'll discuss two important issues in this chapter. The first is how to assess the stewardship culture in the congregation. The second is a simple method to summarize the congregation's giving records to reveal giving patterns and trends. These two issues will help determine the potential for the success of a congregation's stewardship programs.

I. A Favorable or Unfavorable Giving Climate?

In many congregations a board member is assigned the task of recruiting stewardship or pledge-drive volunteers. This task is often accepted grudgingly because this is viewed as a role parishioners do not accept enthusiastically. Rather, they have to be talked into it against their better judgment.

Parishioners who are asked to become stewardship volunteers need to assess the current climate toward stewardship in the congregation. This is particularly important if they intend to challenge low-level and same-level giving. By asking a few simple questions before accepting the job, potential volunteers can ensure that taking on stewardship roles will be a rewarding experience for them—and for the minister, the congregation's leadership, and the congregation as a whole.

In many congregations, once a board member has recruited stewardship volunteers, the board views its role in stewardship as complete. Volunteers are on their own after that. This assumption is not acceptable. It is not the job of the stewardship chair alone, nor of members of the stewardship committee themselves, to devise methods that will supposedly (and somehow magically) persuade a reluctant congregation to give more.

The job of influencing the congregation toward increased generosity is that of the clergy and lay leadership. Their role is similar to the roles they would play in any other major church initiative. For example, the minister and board would not recruit parishioners to conduct a new outreach effort, then have no comment and remain completely uninvolved. The minister and the church leadership set the tone and make decisions on overall church policy. The job of stewardship volunteers is to carry out that policy, with the leadership's unqualified, enthusiastic, and visible support.

Church boards are often conservative, however, and cautious about accepting new ideas. Stewardship volunteers may believe the approach recommended in this book would be effective in their congregation, but some members of the board may disagree. Board members who are low-level donors may be particularly resistant. Telltale signs are such comments as "Maybe we shouldn't jump into something new right away," or "People in the congregation are struggling financially, so this wouldn't be a good time to bring up giving more to the church."

If the congregation's leadership is hesitant toward the idea of increased generosity, these four simple questions will help determine their views toward charitable giving:

- What is their current view of charitable giving in the church?
- Do they believe parishioners are giving what they should? What they can?
- Do they believe generosity is a core value for a religious person?
- How do they believe the congregation would react to calls for increased generosity?

If the board is reluctant to address these issues, it may be too early to introduce new stewardship concepts to the congregation. If stewardship leaders are truly committed to increasing generosity in the congregation, they might ask the board to appoint an ad-hoc committee to study these issues further and to seek additional input from the leadership and members.

If a congregation has to go this route, the ad-hoc committee should include a number of high-level donors. Why? Because a group of low-level donors may not wish to change the congregation's established giving patterns. The goal of the ad-hoc committee is to provide opportunities for parishioners at all giving levels to express their views.

If an ad-hoc group engages the congregation in discussion, it would be awkward for anyone to argue publicly against being more generous, and for being miserly. Parishioners who are opposed are more likely to express hesitation. These are stalling tactics similar to those mentioned above, and may be used by congregants who give little and have no intention of increasing their gifts to the church. The status quo in many congregations is a powerful force. Do not underestimate its staying power.

Parishioners may want to know what the church would do with extra money that might be raised. The leadership of the congregation can support the stewardship effort by having ready answers for such inquiries. It is not the job of the stewardship committee to determine spending priorities.

Moving Ahead

Whether or not an ad-hoc committee is formed, I believe the support of the governing body can be secured. Stewardship volunteers can accomplish this aim by introducing the idea of increased generosity in advance to a select number of board members, including the chair. There is wisdom in the saying, "If you don't know how a group is going to vote, you'll probably lose." Seek support from board members who are generous donors and committed to the church. Church boards avoid confrontation if at all possible. If a board member who is a low-level donor gets the floor and states that increased generosity will not work in the congregation, other board members may not challenge this view even if they disagree with it. Don't allow the voices of the least-generous people on the board (and in the congregation) to deter you from the goal.

My experience in working with congregations is that board members will suggest variations on the theme of leading generous lives, but will approve the idea. Once board members have agreed to the concept as leaders of the congregation, they are likely to consider it in their own lives.

Note well: The minister and members of the board need to support only two concepts. The first is the idea that religious people should be challenged to lead more generous lives. Second, the stewardship committee will exercise its best judgment in the management of the pledge drive. Members of the stewardship committee do not have to attend board meetings to seek approval for the content of stewardship letters, the design of return envelopes, and other day-to-day issues of conducting the pledge drive.

How Stewardship Volunteers Are Viewed by the Congregation

In my own church, I have been blessed by discovering parishioners for whom charitable giving is an integral part of their religious lives. I believe stewardship volunteers in most congregations will have similar experiences. Sometimes in the supermarket or elsewhere around town, parishioners I hardly know have told me how pleased they are that our congregation is approaching stewardship in a positive way. They speak animatedly about the influence that charitable giving can have on both our religious and personal lives. It takes only one such person to make being a stewardship volunteer a memorable experience.

The stewardship committee may, in fact, hear from very few such people. Low-level giving may be the norm in your congregation, and many parishioners are not inclined to give more. They may be upset that you've raised the issue. Lyle Schaller, in *44 Ways to Expand the Financial Base of Your Congregation,* writes, "Accept the fact that [as a pledge drive volunteer] you may be rebuffed, ignored, defeated, snubbed, rejected, vanquished, crushed, outvoted, and discredited in your attempts to increase the financial base of your congregation." Schaller then jokes that the reason for including 44 ways to raise money is that if the first 43 fail, it is unlikely that anyone would miss in 44 consecutive attempts![1]

In leading the pledge drive, stewardship committee members may find that their relationship with fellow parishioners changes. For example, the stewardship committee has access to pledge records, and members will discover for the first time what their friends and neighbors give to the church. Some may wonder whether such access is a good thing. For example, after leading the pledge drive in my own congregation, I sensed a distance from a number of fellow parishioners. Occasionally, at the supermarket I would encounter a low-level donor, nondonor, or member who hadn't paid a pledge. It was amusing to watch their maneuvers, turning grocery carts around in mid-aisle and heading the other way to avoid me. I was never sure if I was the one who should be embarrassed because I emphasized higher-level giving, or if they should be, because I had discovered a part of their private lives they would rather have hidden.

Douglas John Hall writes in *The Steward* that unpleasant side effects can result for the brave souls who urge parishioners to change their giving habits. "Often, such persons [who lead stewardship drives] are secretly and sometimes not so secretly scorned," Hall writes. "Often they suffer acutely because they know they are scorned."[2]

Potential volunteers need to think carefully about leading stewardship initiatives if they believe that personal criticism or the negative attitudes of parishioners will be an issue. I feel that my friendships with some parishioners have diminished. I find that some people are less likely to engage me in conversation because they do not agree with the approach the stewardship program has taken. I suspect that others who keep their distance have no interest in increasing their giving, and no intention of discussing the subject.

An Idea That Worked Well

Let me provide a specific example of how a stewardship committee and a church board worked together to create a more positive climate for stewardship. I once worked with a congregation of about 500 members. This church conducted its pledge drive in the spring, during March and April. In late June all pledging households received a printed card in the mail, thanking them for their pledge. Everyone received the same card, regardless of the amount given.

The stewardship committee did not believe that the generic note-card appropriately acknowledged parishioners' pledges. Seeking something more personalized, they proceeded with confidence in devising a new approach. The next spring, they changed the process. First, they acknowledged all pledges within five days of receipt, instead of months later. Second, parishioners received a personalized letter on the church's letterhead stationery. The letter began with the sentence, "We are writing to thank you for your pledge of $_____ to the church." Each letter stated the amount of the pledge. The letter summarized in a positive manner a variety of successful programs underway in the church, and discussed the value of charitable giving in helping congregants lead more meaningful religious lives. Each letter was signed by the senior minister, the associate minister, the director of religious education, the music director, the board chair, and the stewardship committee chair.

The new acknowledgment letter had an impact on the giving culture of the congregation in four important ways. First, the personalized signatures meant that for the first time ever, six church leaders knew what parishioners gave to the church. Second, when the minister, staff, and key church leaders next saw parishioners, either in church or elsewhere, they were able to acknowledge personally a member's support of the church. Donors can never be thanked too often. These face-to-face encounters reaffirm a donor's belief that he or she did the right thing. Third, by adding their signatures to the letter, church leaders indicated their support of the stewardship committee and the direction the pledge drive was taking.

Fourth, the letter communicated to low-level donors that their lack of support for the church was known by the church's leadership. This is a sensitive issue. Some readers may be concerned about people of lesser means who are unable to contribute as much as wealthier parishioners. Would their awareness that church leaders know the amount of their gifts or pledges embarrass them?

It is important to distinguish the difference between income level and giving level. A small gift does not necessarily connote a lack of spiritual commitment. Churchgoers of modest incomes often give in proportions equal to or greater than those with higher incomes. Thus it is important to acknowledge parishioners of modest means who give in proportion to their income or assets.

If the stewardship committee adopts an acknowledgment system using personalized letters, low-income donors who are generous to the church may be recognized and acknowledged for their generosity for the first time ever. I believe that a personalized acknowledgment letter does not penalize low-income parishioners who give in proportion to their means. I believe it rewards them. I also believe that parishioners of modest means who contribute generously are elevated in the esteem of church leaders.

Complaints about church leaders knowing the amount that parishioners pledge are likely to come from higher-income donors who contribute small amounts. Do not let complaints from low-level donors thwart your efforts. The least generous members of the congregation should not determine the church's policy toward charitable giving.

At the conclusion of the pledge drive, the stewardship committee received only one complaint about the new acknowledgment letter. It was from a woman who quietly told the stewardship chair that she would prefer the amount of her gift to be known by fewer people. I highly recommend the personalized acknowledgment letter. It is one simple way to begin creating more positive attitudes toward creating generous congregations, and highlighting the important role charitable giving plays in developing our spiritual lives.

I believe parishioners derive great pleasure when they make charitable gifts in appropriate proportion to their incomes. People who give generously to the church take a greater sense of ownership in the congregation. They feel comfortable in church. It is a place that holds great meaning for them—where they have made a sizable commitment. They are often held in high regard by others and usually have great respect for the clergy. They often take leadership roles in congregational life. Stewardship efforts in the congregation should foster positive, enduring attitudes toward giving. This is your goal—not just asking people for money.

The decision to change from the generic printed card to the personalized letter in this church was made by the stewardship committee. The action was not brought to the board for approval. I suspect that if the issue of changing from a printed card to a personalized letter had come before the board for a vote, it would have been defeated. But the stewardship committee members already knew they could proceed with the pledge drive in confidence, using their best judgment.

My comments are not intended to encourage stewardship committees to withhold information from the governing body about how the pledge drive will be conducted. The role of the board is to set policy, not to manage the pledge drive.

Take Things in Sequence

Once the stewardship committee has secured the support of the minister and the board, the next step is for the leadership to introduce committee members at the Sunday worship service (if this is the appropriate time and place in your faith tradition). This introduction should be made on two consecutive Sundays when attendance is expected to be high. Both the minister and the board chair should speak enthusiastically about the committee leadership and the direction the stewardship effort will take. The stewardship committee has their enthusiastic and unqualified support.

In addition to public announcements, the next two church newsletters should carry similar endorsements, preferably from respected members of the congregation. Included in this group should be a number of the congregation's largest contributors. This inclusion will lessen the possibility of an unpleasant surprise—a church pillar opposing a new stewardship approach after its announcement.

The First Challenge

Let's hope the minister and members of the board are already generous donors. If so, the pledge drive will begin from a position of strength. As we have discussed, if the minister and members of the board are already in the top 20 percent of donors, they are likely to increase their giving, especially if they believe it will improve the chances of a successful pledge drive. Its success will reflect well on their leadership.

If the minister and members of the board contribute little to the church, their giving level will undermine the stewardship committee's attempts to create a congregation of generous people. It is not the committee's job, however, to solicit charitable contributions from the minister or board. The board, along with the minister, should discuss at the earliest opportunity the level of support they will provide.

This does not mean that individual board members must disclose the amount of their own pledges or gifts. Rather, the board should determine the total dollar amount or a percentage of the church's operating budget they will collectively give for the coming year. The board chair then distributes pledge cards, and members are asked to return them within one week. The board chair provides regular updates, saying, "We agreed as a board that we would contribute $____ to the church. To date, we have received $____ from _____ members."

The board chair or executive committee is responsible for gathering pledges from board members and the minister, and for meeting the challenge they set for themselves. If the minister and members of the board are low-level donors, the board chair should be informed of the total amount previously given. A higher dollar figure can then be determined, one that will set an example for the congregation as a whole.

The amount that a board is able to contribute will, of course, vary from congregation to congregation. The amount given will be less in a church in an economically depressed area than a congregation in an affluent neighborhood. In America, most households give more to their churches and synagogues than to any other charitable cause. I believe the church should be the charitable priority of the minister and every board member during their time of service to the congregation.

What Will You Give?

By now, members of the stewardship committee may realize that their own contributions are important as well. Parishioners do not need to be wealthy to lead the pledge drive. It would be a mistake, in fact, for stewardship roles to be viewed as volunteer opportunities that only wealthy members of the congregation can enjoy. But stewardship volunteers need to make "leadership gifts"—amounts that are generous in proportion to their means.

Those who serve on the stewardship committee should contribute in proportion to what they are asking the congregation to contribute. A high-income, low-level donor can be a devastating presence on the stewardship committee and can destroy the respect and credibility that members have worked so hard to build. Do not let this happen! The minister, members of the board, stewardship committee members, and you—all church leaders need to make generous pledges to the church.

I realize that some parishioners may be struggling financially or facing financial hardship. These people should not be excluded from stewardship opportunities, either to give or to serve as volunteers. It may, in fact, be very important to a person's self-esteem to continue supporting the church to the extent possible, and to take an active role in church life.

Other Things the Stewardship Committee Will Need

The stewardship committee requires an adequate budget to conduct the pledge drive effectively. Usually costs are modest and include such items as printing and stationery expenses for a pledge bulletin, pledge cards, and return envelopes, and the cost of postage. Some churches provide light refreshments after church. Others hold catered fellowship dinners, which can be expensive. Whatever the tradition in your congregation, the stewardship committee requires adequate funds to do the job well. If more money is needed than currently budgeted, ask for an increase. Don't let the traditional budget process allocate a minimal amount to the stewardship committee, which might result in stewardship initiatives being less than first-rate.

Kickoff Sunday also needs to be put on the church calendar, and arrangements made for pulpit announcements the following few weeks. In most congregations the minister, choir director, and religious-education staff plan Sunday services eight to 12 months in advance. Make sure you get

Kickoff Sunday on the church calendar as early as possible. Also arrange for articles in the church newsletter well in advance.

II. Current Giving: Where Are You Starting From?

Two commonly held beliefs persist in many congregations. The first is that parishioners don't have much to give. The second is that people are already giving as much as they possibly can. Both are myths. Don McClanen, former director of the Ministry of Money program, provides a powerful guide to help American churchgoers determine what they have in comparison to others in the world. There are five levels:

- *Poorest of the poor.* People with no family, job, housing, health care, or even a place to die.
- *Ordinary poor.* People with limited access to income, housing, food, or health care.
- *Ordinary wealthy.* People with access to jobs, housing, food, health care, and transportation.
- *Wealthiest of the wealthy.* People with more than sufficient income, housing, investments, and possessions.
- *The ultra-wealthy.* The billionaires. A phenomenon of new import in the [19]80s and [19]90s.[3]

When I use this chart in groups, most people are surprised to find that they fall into the wealthy category. Usually middle-class families, the majority of churchgoers in America, do not view themselves in this way. They tend to compare themselves to the wealthiest families in the community rather than to their economic peers and thus consider themselves worse off economically. This chart provides an excellent starting place to determine what people in your congregation have. It challenges the perception that they have little to give.

Assessing the Congregation's Giving Potential

How much do people in your congregation actually have? What is their capacity to give? An important starting point in answering these questions is determining the congregation's gross income. There are a number of ways to estimate gross income, ranging from fairly specific calculations to broad estimates. On the more specific end of the spectrum, salary surveys and professional literature about income levels in all professions are readily available. It is a simple matter to locate an accurate salary estimate for the average doctor, lawyer, nurse, electrician, plumber, truck driver, civil servant, computer programmer, social worker, general laborer, or any other occupation.

Some stewardship committees gather salary surveys and estimate income on a household-by-household basis. What might be the income of Dr. Smith, a heart surgeon; Mrs. Jones, a preschool teacher; Mr. Taylor, who works for the highway department; or the Johnsons, a retired couple? Some congregations may view this exercise as an invasion of privacy. The broader measures spelled out below may be more appropriate.

The salary-per-household method is a simple and accurate way to estimate gross household income and giving potential for the congregation as a whole. Let's take an even number of $10 million as an estimated gross income for a congregation, for ease in calculation. It sounds like a lot of money, but it actually applies to a congregation of only 200 households with an average income of $50,000. If church members gave 1.7 percent of their gross incomes (the current average per household contribution in America to all charitable causes), that would amount to a $170,000 annual pledge drive. For a tithing congregation, the goal might reach or exceed $1 million—a big difference!

Estimating gross income provides a guide to what a congregation can give. The stewardship committee should share the figures on gross income with the congregation. Parishioners are likely to be surprised at how large this number is. A simple calculation like gross congregational income is one of a number of ways to dispel the myth that middle- and upper-middle-class parishioners cannot be generous because they don't have money to give.

Other methods may be used to calculate gross congregational income. In any congregation, there are likely to be a certain number of households in different income ranges. The following is a guide to incomes in the United States:

- The lowest 20 percent of Americans have a family income of $0 to $19,970.
- The next 20 percent have household incomes from $19,070 to $32,985.

- The third 20 percent have household incomes of $32,985 to $48,985.
- The fourth 20 percent have household incomes of $49,985 to $72,260.
- The next 15 percent have household incomes of $72,260 to $123,000.
- The top 5 percent have household incomes of $123,000 and higher.

Using this method, members of the stewardship committee can estimate how many families in the congregation might fit into each category. For example, if 20 families fell into the $32,985-to-$48,985 range, that calculation would be: 20 x $40,000 (a midpoint), or $800,000 in gross income.

Another method is to find the per-capita and median incomes for your city or town. This method assumes that most people in the congregation come from the surrounding area. Per-capita incomes can be found in such government publications as *The Survey of Current Business*, or *Labor Statistics*, or *A Statistical Abstract of the United States*. All three publications can be found in public libraries. By multiplying the per-capita income by the number of wage-earners in the congregation, one can approximate the congregation's gross income.

Median incomes can also be found in *Sales and Marketing Management*, available in local libraries. A combination of all these sources might yield the most accurate assessment of a congregation's gross income. In my experience, once the concept of gross congregational income has been introduced to the congregation, members are eager to know what that figure adds up to.

Members of your church probably have no idea of the gross congregational income. Furthermore, if it is a goodly sum while the annual giving is paltry, these comparisons will demonstrate the point that religious people can be called to lead more generous lives than they do now.

Gross income figures, however, should not be used to ask for an across-the-board increase in giving. Stewardship leaders should not say, "Overall giving in this congregation is only 1.5 percent, and it should be 2 percent." This approach is likely to be perceived as scolding the congregation. Gross income figures are just one element in building a case for increased support—not a damning indictment that parishioners give too little. As we have discussed in previous chapters, some people are generous, others less so. Averages and percentages are broad measures only. They are helpful in completing the larger portrait of giving in your congregation, but they do not apply to individual households equally.

What Have Your Members Given in Recent Years?

To assess the potential success of the pledge drive, it is imperative that the stewardship committee know where it is starting from. The essential starting point is an analysis of giving figures going back as many years as possible. Of particular importance is what the congregation has contributed over the past three to five years. Is the amount parishioners give to the church increasing or decreasing? Is the number of pledging households increasing or decreasing? Is membership increasing or decreasing?

Once these figures are determined, the stewardship committee should inform the minister, the church leadership, and members of the congregation, so that everyone will know whether the church is on a rising or ebbing tide. As a stewardship volunteer, you need to know if you have inherited a positive giving situation, or if congregational giving is on a downturn. It makes a difference in how you will proceed. A simple format such as that on the following page can be used.

Many churches would report only two figures: Total giving had increased from the previous year, from $243,000 to $249,000. The average pledge had decreased slightly, from $943 to $933—certainly no cause for alarm. Things look fine in the church!

But if you were going to lead the pledge drive in this congregation, what assessment would you make? What trends do these numbers indicate? Let's take a closer look.

First, total giving has indeed increased by $6,000, or 2.5 percent. Taking inflation into account, the church has the same purchasing power as the year before. Thus, the church will be unable to undertake any new initiatives, and staff members will not receive even a cost-of-living adjustment. How is this likely to affect staff members' morale and their enthusiasm for working at the church, and their attitude toward parishioners who give very little?

Next, the number of new-member households is listed as 29. But there are only nine new pledging households. A closer examination of the donor list indicates that a few families have moved away, resulting in a loss of pledging households. But the figures also reveal that 14 of 29 new-member households were nondonors. This statistic indicates that the membership committee is ineffective in setting giving expectations for new members—definitely cause for concern.

Third, a significant number of same-level donors are found at all levels, but especially among those giving less than $1,000. Have these parishioners

Total amount pledged:	This year $249,200	Last year $243,675
Pledging households	264	261
Pledge amount	**This year**	**Last year**
$15,000+	1	1
$10,000—$15,000	2	2
$7,500—$9,999	0	0
$5,000—$7,499	3	3
$2,500—$4,999	12	11
$2,000—$2,499	13	11
$1,500—$1,999	26	25
$1,000—$1,499	31	29
$750—$999	18	17
$500—$749	36	34
$250—$499	41	44
$100—$249	27	26
$1—$99	12	13
Nondonors	42	45

Top 7 donors (3%) pledged $60,000 (25% of total).
Top 27 donors (10%) pledged $108,000 (44% of total).
Largest category: 41 households, pledged between $250 and $499.
Second-largest category: 42 households are non-donors.
Average pledge of those who pledged: $1,122 ($1,128 last year).
Average pledge including nondonors: $943 ($933 last year).
Median (half above, half below) pledge for the entire congregation: between
      $475 and $500 (similar to last year).
Average pledge (top 50% of total dollars pledged): $3,315 (37 donors).
Average pledge (bottom 50% of total dollars pledged): $545 (227 donors).
New member households: 29.

risen to their highest level of giving, at least to date? Their giving patterns may have been established over many years and may be difficult to change.

Fourth, while the average pledge has risen, the median pledge remains between $475 and $500. Half the congregation gives less than $10 per week to the church. Do the leaders of your congregation find this an acceptable level of financial support among middle-class members?

Finally, the median gift for the top half of dollars pledged ($125,000) is $3,315, from 37 households. The median gift for the remaining half of dollars pledged (also $125,000) is $502, from 227 households. Thus, it could be said that 37 donors carry the church financially, while 227 donors are carried by the church. Speaking of being carried by the church, a large number of households remain nondonors.

I believe that congregations should be provided the facts and figures that represent giving in the church. Parishioners are probably unaware of these figures and trends. They will also be curious to learn where they stand relative to fellow parishioners in terms of their giving to the church.

The figures above represent a typical pattern of giving, perhaps but not necessarily with the exception of a high level of nondonors. These figures are from a congregation in a community with a stable population, so the patterns are similar to previous years. Churches in transient areas will experience a higher level of nonrenewal among members. There is not a "normal" rate of renewal among donor households. Parishioners come and go in unpredictable patterns. The stewardship committee needs to compare renewal and nonrenewal rates over as many years as possible, to determine whether they are rising or falling.

In the figures presented above, this congregation had used the annual operating budget as the centerpiece of the pledge drive for many years. Parishioners were conditioned to give toward paying the church's bills. The low median pledge, less than $10 per week, suggests that at least half the people in the congregation believe the church pays its bills, so they have little reason to give more.

One issue not reflected in the numbers alone is who these donors actually are. In this congregation, as in many, two of the top three donors are in their 80s. Given the low rate of pledging among new members, it would take almost 100 newcomers to equal the giving of these two elderly households.

These calculations are imperative to get a clear picture of your congregation's giving patterns. In compiling the gift chart, the top figure should be the highest pledge or gift the church has received. Then list the remaining gifts in order. *Do not exclude nondonors*! The list is not complete if only pledging households are included. It is extremely important to know how many households do not pledge, and whether this number is increasing or decreasing.

Given the preceding analysis, would you lead the pledge drive in this congregation? At this point, your answer might be "Maybe." Your decision would depend on the reaction of the minister and the congregation's leadership to the figures presented. Many churches are slow to react to issues that do not pose an immediate threat. The minister and members of the board might believe that so long as the total amount pledged remains the same or slightly higher, the church is fine. If this is their view, then just about anyone can lead the pledge drive by repeating what has been done in previous years. Eventually, the elderly donors will die, and the church will be faced with a financial crisis with which it will deal at that time—perhaps successfully, perhaps not.

A major item on the essential checklist is what the minister and the board expect from the pledge drive. If the total amount pledged remains about the same, is that sufficient? Do church leaders wish to increase giving? If so, would they anticipate an increase of 3 percent, 5 percent, 10 percent, or more? Will church leaders support the idea of engaging the congregation in serious discussion about low-level and same-level giving? Will the leadership challenge members of the church to lead more generous lives? Will the leadership ask members to forego the purchase of consumer items, or make financial sacrifices for the benefit of the church or other charitable causes? You need to know the answers to these questions, and the commitment of the congregation's leadership to these issues, before signing on to lead any stewardship initiatives in church.

Do Parishioners Pay Their Pledges?

One additional figure the stewardship committee needs to know is the percentage of pledges that are paid. Churches should receive 95 percent or more of pledges. This level allows a 5 percent margin for people who move away during the church year or who have financial difficulties. Anything below 95 percent can signal the beginning of a serious problem.

The most immediate way to increase pledge redemption rates is to examine the church's system for mailing pledge statements or reminders. Parishioners should receive reminders at least quarterly, preferably every other month. The statement should be accompanied by a cheerful note from the minister or a lay leader. If parishioners receive reminders on a timely basis and begin paying their pledges early in the year, they are more likely to pay in full. If parishioners fall behind in their pledge payments, they may feel guilty or embarrassed and not pledge again for the coming year. Make sure parishioners who fall behind in their pledge payments know that they can contact the church treasurer or other sympathetic soul in the church leadership, even if by note, so they won't feel embarrassed when coming to church.

Keep an eye out for parishioners who fall behind in their pledges. If you don't see them in church for a while, notify the minister. You don't want financial difficulties to result in members leaving the church. This may be a time when the church could assist struggling members in a particularly important way.

Where to Go from Here

The final chapter of this book puts all the issues we've discussed into a time frame, a month-to-month schedule of how stewardship efforts might unfold in a congregation. These guidelines will provide a congregation with many options from which to choose. They will help volunteers initiate an effective stewardship program, ensure that efforts stay on track, and provide guidance throughout the church year.

CHAPTER 8

Implementing a 12-Month Stewardship Program

Virginia Howard was treasurer of a large urban congregation. Among her responsibilities was recording the cash and checks collected in the Sunday offering. This weekly task was a reminder of her late husband's view of contributing to the church. Her husband was a banker who handled the family's finances during his lifetime. Virginia would often say, "My husband divided the bills into two categories—those we had to pay, and those we chose to pay. In a category by itself, the first check he wrote wasn't to pay a bill—it was to the church. This made him very happy." Now that she was widowed, she carried on this tradition and encouraged other parishioners to consider the same view.

Creating Positive Attitudes Toward Giving Year 'Round

Fund-raising consultant Ashley Hale writes about money in a similar way, using a type of happiness scale. "Some money is sad money, some is happy money," he writes. "Sad money is paid as a duty or a penalty. Taxes, debt-payments, fines—these are paid with sad money. Unfortunately, many church members respond to stewardship appeals with sad money."[1]

In contrast, Hale offers an example of happy money as that used "when you spend more than you should on a loved one's birthday present. Happy-money giving is generous giving. Members of a congregation who give happy money will get along better with each other and love their church more than a congregation that is giving sad money."[2]

Beyond the notion of cheerful giving, another dimension of stewardship should also be conveyed to the congregation. In his essay "Philanthropy in Short Fiction," Joseph Harmon, a librarian at Indiana University, writes,

"From the stories collected here, one discovers that philanthropy is not for the faint-of-heart. It can result in its practitioners being transformed in ways they neither expected nor desired."

"Philanthropy exacts a human cost," Harmon continues. "It pulls us out of our self-imposed, self-defined existence and opens us up to the unknown. It makes us vulnerable. We are no longer dealing with ideas or philosophies, but with people and with basic human needs, such as survival and pride and relationships and mutual responsibilities."[3]

These views of charitable giving—bringing happiness, yet with the possibility of opening up the unknown—are but two of the many concepts that can create a compelling stewardship program in congregations. Stewardship education is an integral part of church life because it instills in us one of the core values of the spiritual life. As we strengthen our faith, we need continually to reexamine our views about money in church and in our everyday lives. I believe churches can create thoughtful, effective, and powerful stewardship initiatives that will engage parishioners over the course of their entire lives. This objective requires stewardship programs that carry on throughout the church year. Talking about money for only a few weeks during the annual pledge drive is a formula for maintaining the status quo.

From the Pews Up

In the preface I wrote that if clergy and lay leaders didn't know how parishioners viewed the use of money in their lives, the church would be at a disadvantage in asking them for it. Many congregations have difficulty discussing money. When the subject of money does come up in church, it is usually in the context of asking parishioners for it. Money discussions are almost always led by the minister or lay leaders. Rarely do people in the pews have an opportunity or a forum in which to express their own views.

The month-by-month overview that follows is based on obtaining a wide range of parishioners' views on how stewardship should be handled in the congregation. By involving church members more directly in the stewardship process, you lay the foundation to create a congregation of generous people.

This guide is not based on a calendar or fiscal year. It begins at the time when parishioners might be asked to consider stewardship responsibilities, regardless of the month or season. In the example that follows, the pledge-drive kickoff does not come until the 11th month. All issues described in the 12-month guide are discussed in greater detail in previous chapters.

The First Month

Timing. Many congregations conclude the annual pledge drive in the fall or spring, then wait months before recruiting new leadership. A couple of months is often viewed as ample time for new volunteers to prepare the pledge drive. A stewardship program requires a great deal of thought and preparation. Many church leaders have not been involved in stewardship programs and frequently underestimate how much time and effort are required.

Volunteers might be recruited in September to lead a pledge drive that begins in November, or maybe next week! If you or others in the congregation intend to make changes in the church's stewardship program or implement the recommendations in this book, two months (or one week) is not sufficient time. It is possible, however, to pick and choose a few ideas that can be introduced on short notice, and take a long-range view about others. Some of the recommendations that follow may also be compressed into a shorter time period. Introducing the concept of becoming generous people is one that should not be delayed, regardless of how little time you have to prepare.

Some congregations have small stewardship committees, maybe only a person or two. Other congregations recruit a large number of volunteers in varying capacities. Many churches have frequent turnover among stewardship volunteers, while others have a few stalwarts who may have been on board for many years. Parishioners who assume leadership roles will need to assess the strengths and weaknesses of the current stewardship committee. A good starting place might be to clarify the difference between fund-raising and stewardship.

Incoming volunteers may find a group of current volunteers who are eager to try new ideas and methods. Or they may find one or more people who are hesitant about new initiatives or resistant to changes being considered. Incoming volunteers will need to find a middle ground between new initiatives the existing committee will embrace, and those that will take more time to implement.

Assessment. Begin by assessing the congregation's giving patterns for as many previous years as possible. Compile a list of the number of gifts at each dollar level. (A sample is included in chapter 7.) From these figures, you can then calculate whether the following measures are *increasing* or *decreasing:*

- The total amount given.
- The number of contributing households.
- The membership of the church.
- New-member giving.
- The number of nondonors.

Some congregations require a pledge or gift "of record" for a new-comer to become a member. In some congregations the gift of record is a minimal amount, such as $25. In other congregations the amount is unspecified. Thus, it is not possible to have a member who is a nondonor. If this is the case in your congregation, the stewardship committee should list the number of households that make the minimum gift necessary for membership in the church.

If the number of donor households and the total amount contributed are increasing, current stewardship programs have a record of success upon which you can build. If total giving has decreased or the number of pledging households has decreased, implementing a new stewardship approach may be much more complicated. It is essential that stewardship volunteers know where they are starting from. For example, it is possible for a church to raise about the same amount in a given year or two, yet have an eroding donor base. Do not allow a treasurer or financial secretary to withhold the congregation's giving figures. Congregational giving trends need to be clearly identified.

The Second Month

Figures in hand, the stewardship committee should make an appearance before the governing body and the minister to get their reactions to the congregation's giving history.

Interpretation and Reactions

Church leaders may not have seen figures in this format before. If only an average pledge has been reported over the years, some church leaders may believe that most parishioners give about the same amount. The figures in your congregation will portray skewed giving, and some board members may be surprised at the sizable number of people who give very little. A common reaction might be, "Well, people who are giving less will just have to give more!" As we have seen, this approach will not work, and the stewardship chair will probably have to explain why.

The reactions of the minister and the board are very important. If the amount given by the congregation is the same or has increased slightly over the past few years, church leaders may view this level as acceptable. They may believe there is no reason to change the stewardship program or consider any of the recommendations brought forth. If so, the stewardship committee will not have the full support of church leaders for new stewardship initiatives. If this is the case, one might want to reconsider the decision to provide leadership for stewardship programs in the congregation.

Seeking Support

If giving has decreased in recent years, the minister and the board will be keenly interested in new stewardship possibilities. Even if giving is stable or slightly increasing, perceptive ministers and lay leaders may realize that there are weak spots in the system (for example, elderly people being among the largest donors) and wish to consider new methods.

The unanimous, unqualified, and visible support of the minister and the board are critical to the success of stewardship programs in your congregation—not just during the pledge drive, but throughout the year. The support of the congregation's leadership includes stewardship volunteers being introduced during Sunday worship, if that practice is acceptable in your faith tradition. If not, introductions should occur at other church gatherings. Support should also include notices in the newsletter, preferably written by members of the congregation who enjoy great respect and admiration.

Financial Support

The minister and members of the board should make generous pledges or gifts in accordance with their means. All stewardship committee members should do likewise. Parishioners cannot be asked to do what leaders are unwilling to do. Generous gifts from the church's leadership will set an important example for others, which will help create favorable attitudes toward giving throughout the congregation.

The Third And Fourth Months

The stewardship committee now needs to initiate a discussion about charitable giving with members of the congregation.

Engaging the Congregation

The stewardship committee probably does not know a great deal about why parishioners contribute the amounts they do. Some well-to-do families may give generously while others contribute very little. Parishioners of average means may also make gifts either large or small. Some active parishioners may not give at all. Some people who have not been to church for many years may continue to make annual gifts. All church leaders would benefit from a greater understanding of the range of attitudes toward charitable giving among parishioners.

Opening the Dialogue

The stewardship committee can begin the dialogue on stewardship in a number of ways. If pulpit announcements are deemed appropriate, you might announce that informal stewardship discussions will be held after the service for the next few weeks. The church newsletter can be used in a similar manner. Some congregations include the subject of stewardship in adult-education programs.

Don't expect people to line up at the door. As we have discussed, 80 percent of parishioners are unlikely to increase their giving significantly. They are not going to attend a meeting that challenges them to do something they don't want to do. However, it is still necessary to inform the congregation frequently that stewardship discussions are underway.

The stewardship committee will need to engage members of the congregation, rather than waiting for them to respond to pulpit announcements or newsletter blurbs. One effective method is to summarize a variety of stewardship issues on a page or two (a sample is provided below) and mail copies to the top 20 percent of donors in your congregation, requesting their feedback. These donors are usually among the most committed to the church, and wish the church to prosper. You will hear back from them.

The importance of this dialogue cannot be understated, as two particular benefits accrue. First, the stewardship committee and church leaders will learn a great deal about how parishioners view money in their lives and in the church. After hearing what parishioners have to say on the subject of money, the stewardship committee can report something like the following to the congregation:

> We have heard many thoughts about stewardship from members of this congregation. Some believe the church sets standards that are too low in terms of what parishioners should give. The church should provide more education and guidance, especially to newcomers. Some senior members of the congregation who have contributed to the church for decades and decades wonder if younger generations will follow their example. We've also heard that with everything costing more these days, parishioners feel they have less to give to the church. These are but three issues we will discuss further in this year's pledge drive.

Stewardship programs should be based on the attitudes and beliefs of church members. Stewardship is a matter of building on dialogue with members of your congregation. This dialogue would certainly include favorable attitudes toward charitable giving; parishioners who exhibit a strong commitment to the faith; and those who set positive examples by their words and deeds. The dialogue will also uncover questions, doubts, and misunderstandings about stewardship and the way we view money in church and in our lives. All views and opinions are important ingredients in creating a meaningful dialogue with your congregation.

By encompassing the widest possible range of views, you will address financial issues that have the most significant impact on parishioners' lives. This is much more effective than the stewardship committee's thinking up a theme on its own. Let the congregation determine its own themes. You may not even need a single theme. This is particularly important because the issues you are identifying are complex, and could not possibly be addressed adequately in a single year. They will carry over from year to year, resulting in more consistent, ongoing stewardship initiatives.

Second, engaging members of your congregation in dialogue (see next section for recommendations) helps clarify the role of the stewardship committee. It is not the job of the stewardship committee alone to discuss charitable giving in the church. Rather, the committee serves as a liaison between the congregational leadership and the people in the pews. The role of the stewardship committee should be conveyed to the congregation along these lines:

> Here are the hopes and dreams members of this congregation have articulated to us; here is how the leadership of the church plans to carry them out; and here is how money is used in this congregation. The stewardship committee's role is not to view parishioners as reluctant donors, needing to be convinced of the value of giving to the church, or harangued into giving money. As a congregation we've already decided that our goals are worthy, and deserving of our financial support in full measure. The role of the stewardship committee is to create the climate that will enable you to make charitable giving a meaningful part of your life, in church and in your day-to-day lives. Our goal is to provide enlightening examples from our faith and others, to help members of this congregation deepen their spiritual lives, and for all of us to think and pray about becoming generous people.

Sample Questions and Issues

Many factors will help create a meaningful dialogue with the congregation about the use of money in church and in people's lives. A number of issues, of which parishioners may be unaware, lie beyond the local congregation. I believe these are important, however, to introduce into the conversation.

- Churches exist in an increasingly indifferent and hostile environment. Stephen Carter, a law professor at Yale University, writes: "We have created a culture that presses the religiously faithful to be other than themselves, to act publicly and sometimes privately as though their faith does not matter to them. Many people do not share their religious journeys with others, even in church. For Americans to take their religions seriously is to risk assignment to the lunatic fringe."[4]
- Churches are having a diminishing effect on society. The church's voice seems to be silent on many ethical and moral issues of the times.

- Churches and their members are powerfully affected by an increasingly materialistic society, one that exalts accumulation of material goods.
- Sadly, some churches are becoming less and less distinguishable from other places of commerce and entertainment.
- Churches face ever-increasing competition from TV, movies, sports, and professional organizations of various sorts.
- Churches have less and less to do with people's work lives, economic lives, and the pressures families face day to day.

With the exception of the first comment by Stephen Carter, the issues above have been identified by Robert Wuthnow, director of the Center for the Study of American Religion at Princeton University.[5] Wuthnow believes that churches are literally under siege from the pervasive influence of a consumer-oriented society. While members of your congregation may feel no imminent threat to their church, parishioners are not immune to the effects of the consumer-oriented culture in which we all live.

Church membership, along with charitable giving, has declined for more than 30 years. Some observers believe that America is on an inevitable path to secularism, similar to the changes seen in Great Britain, where only 3 percent of the population attends religious services. The future of the church in America is not secure, and members of local congregations should not be permitted to view their religious communities with complacency, believing that only token gifts are necessary to keep the church open indefinitely. I know of at least seven church buildings near my home, all in vibrant neighborhoods, that no longer exist as religious communities. Two have been turned into restaurants, two are movie theaters, two are condominiums, and one is a karate studio. It saddens me when I drive by these beautiful old church buildings and see them used in these unforeseen ways. I wonder if the congregations that once inhabited these structures ever suspected their eventual fate.

Closer to Home

Numerous issues will be of more immediate consequence to the congregation's leadership and members. These are key to initiating and sustaining effective stewardship programs.

- We are not asking for a pledge. The challenge is to become generous people. How will parishioners react to this challenge?
- Will we lead lives that go against the grain of the prevailing consumer culture? Are we called to lead lives of dedication, commitment and sacrifice?
- Can parishioners be asked to forego the purchase of consumer items, and make larger gifts either to the church or to other causes?
- Stewardship is not just the amount we give to the church, but how we spend all our money. Do we live our lives any differently from our unchurched friends and neighbors?
- What is the church called to do? What is our mission, our sense of common purpose? What would we do with the money if the congregation contributed a larger sum?
- Many churches give from 10 to 15 percent of their budgets to the less fortunate. What is our obligation beyond our own four walls?
- Should parishioners consider the church their primary charitable commitment?
- Should parishioners increase their pledges this year and every year they are members of our religious community?

The Fifth and Sixth Months

By now the stewardship committee will have gathered a variety of opinions and impressions from parishioners regarding money in church and in their lives.

Reporting What You Have Heard to the Congregation

The minister and members of the board will be particularly interested in hearing what you have learned. Using quotes is an effective way to summarize a range of opinions. For example, you might report to the leadership and members of the congregation that you have heard, among other opinions, the following views:

- "The church is one of the most important parts of my life. I give what I can."
- "These are hard times, and most people in the congregation are

struggling financially. You can't ask them for more money. They would be offended."

- "My family and I think and pray about what we should give in return for what we have. This is an important decision for us."
- "I don't believe people in this congregation view stewardship as a means of growing in faith."
- "I think people get the full range of benefits no matter what they give. Maybe people think church is free, or they don't want to pay more for something that already costs less."
- "This congregation talks about money only during the pledge drive. We don't think of giving in terms of generosity. It will be a long time before we can think that way."
- "A lot of people believe the ch rch will be pretty much the same from year to year, so why should they give more?"
- "Few people in this congregation will consider giving more. I think some will be upset if the church stresses increased giving. The church could never ask parishioners to give up something, or make a sacrifice."
- "When the church needs money we can raise it, but just barely."
- "Young people just starting out have little to give."
- "Middle-aged people can't afford to give much because they're paying college tuitions for their kids."
- "We have to remember that many seniors in the church are on fixed incomes and don't have much money to give."
- "If the church had more money, it would just spend it."
- "I think the problem is that people nowadays spend about 10 percent more than they earn, so we struggle just to keep even. I think we should include the church in our household budgets so we get in the habit of giving regularly, and not just give from what's left over after everything else is paid."
- "I think everyone in this congregation could give $100 per month."
- "It would be outrageous if the church set an amount that everyone would be asked to give. If the church asked me for $100 a month, I'd leave!"
- "My family and I are sustained by the church in many ways. We are willing stewards for a religious tradition that celebrates our life together, and pushes us to extend our vision to the broader community."

Where to Go from Here

Without doubt the stewardship committee will gather a variety of conflicting opinions. Some will be heartening, others discouraging. All will provide the opportunity for further discussion. Don't view a negative comment as necessarily a bad thing—it may provide the opportunity to address a problematic or long-standing issue that has impeded effective stewardship in the congregation.

The minister and lay leadership of the congregation will also want to comment on the issues identified by the stewardship committee and the opinions gathered from congregants. Church leaders should be an integral part of the discussion regarding parishioners' attitudes toward money. The involvement of the minister and the board will also increase their ownership of an important aspect of church life. They may find themselves in stewardship discussions with parishioners throughout the year, setting an example that money is not an issue addressed by stewardship volunteers alone.

Use quotations whenever possible. The minister and lay leaders should offer their views, even if they are not in complete agreement. However, the minister and lay leaders should agree on one conclusion—they wholeheartedly support the effort to engage parishioners in the dialogue about money in church and in our lives as the basis of effective stewardship programs.

The Sixth and Seventh Months

The more time available to engage the congregation before the annual pledge drive, the better. If the discussion about money is set in the context of education, exploration, and growth in faith, I do not believe pledge-drive leaders will be criticized for talking too often about money in church.

The stewardship committee should also speak with ministers or stewardship committees from other faith traditions in the community. It will be revealing to learn how giving patterns in your congregation compare with other faith groups in the neighborhood. My small town has Mormon and Assemblies of God churches, both of which seek the tithe from members. These two churches have provided a wealth of examples of charitable giving that I have used in pulpit announcements and in written form. The more church leaders are aware of stewardship practices in religious settings other than their own, the more they will be able to implement effective stewardship programs.

The Real Challenge

As the dialogue continues, church leaders will learn a great deal about how parishioners view money in their lives. The next step is to determine the extent to which the congregation can be challenged to increased generosity. You may feel that some parishioners are willing to consider leading more generous lives, and anticipate how they will react to examining their attitudes toward the acquisition of consumer goods. But you may be uncertain about the attitude of the congregation as a whole. I recommend that the stewardship committee seek counsel from the top 20 percent of donors in the congregation. If they support the proposed stewardship initiatives, proceed with confidence.

Challenging people to lead lives of increased generosity is also a subject that the minister and members of the church board will probably want to discuss. In their book *Behind the Stained Glass Windows*, John and Sylvia Ronsvalle write, "The main thing blocking church support is simply a surpassing urge for more affluent living . . . rival attractions seem to be gaining more of the religious dollar."[6] To what extent will the leadership of your congregation challenge spending on these rival attractions?

Robert Wuthnow, in his book *The Crisis in the Churches: Spiritual Malaise, Fiscal Woe*, writes:

> People go to church and hear nothing that challenges them to live their lives differently from their neighbors who have no interest in religion. Churches have an obligation to challenge people to lead better lives than they would otherwise. That is the toughest business of all.[7]

Your stewardship recommendations may have introduced a more significant issue into the life of the congregation than the minister and church board had expected.

Challenging the urge for more affluent living is a central issue in church stewardship. Will members welcome such a challenge? Will some find it offensive? There will be favorable and unfavorable reactions from members of the congregation and a great silence from many others. This challenge may run contrary to charitable customs and habits that have been held for decades and decades. Don't expect church leaders or parishioners to experience revelations about increased giving overnight. Parishioners need time to think and pray about the issues presented. They are being asked to change their lives in a fundamental way.

Should There Be a Dollar Goal?

Congregations in which the operating budget is the focus of the pledge drive usually set specific dollar goals. If parishioners contribute this amount, the goal will be reached and the church will carry on for another year. Capital campaigns, or giving for restricted purposes, also have specific dollar goals. A certain amount of money is required to build a new building or to repair the organ. There is reason to celebrate when goals have been achieved. Setting a dollar goal is a cardinal rule of fund-raising.

In annual stewardship drives, however, setting a dollar goal might inadvertently limit the congregation's capacity to give, for several reasons. First, a dollar goal would be based on last year's goal, which reinforces same-level giving. Second, if you wish to increase the goal, the congregation's leadership might believe it possible to raise it only by a small percentage. In some congregations, a 5 percent rise might be viewed as the upper limit. A 25 percent increase would be out of the question, even though you might believe such an increase (or even more) is within the congregation's capacity to give.

Third, low-level donors tend to wait and see if the goal is reached. Once the top 20 percent have given a large percentage of the total, low-level donors realize the pledge drive will meet its goal eventually and see no need to reconsider their level of giving.

My conviction is that stewardship committees should enthusiastically articulate the message of generosity and proceed with confidence that parishioners will do the right thing. I recommend not setting a dollar goal. Parishioners will be pleasantly surprised upon discovering they have given more than ever before. Finally, there is one important caveat about dollar goals—don't set a higher goal and then fall short.

The Eighth and Ninth Months

By this time, pledge-drive kickoff may be on the horizon. The stewardship committee now needs to engage the next level of leadership—committee chairs. Always remember that stewardship is not the committee's job alone.

The more people involved, the stronger the belief grows among parishioners that stewardship emanates from the pews, not from the pulpit.

Printing a pledge booklet is an inexpensive and effective means of articulating the hopes and dreams of a congregation. A printed booklet also allows many parishioners' names to be included. My recommendation is that stewardship volunteers contact all committee chairs by letter, and ask them to write a brief article that includes the following:

- A brief description of what the committee does.
- What the committee would like to accomplish in the coming year.
- The estimated cost of the committee's work for the coming year.
- Larger hopes and dreams for future years.
- Names of committee members, including chairs and co-chairs.

For example, one pledge publication that I saw recently included the following: The minister requested funds for an increase in his discretionary fund; the choir director hoped for an aide who would file music; the outreach committee wanted to increase its inner-city programs and requested an additional $10,000; the religious-education committee requested $2,000 more for a new seventh- and eighth-grade curriculum; the high-school youth group requested a $2,500 subsidy for a trip; the adult-education committee asked for money to begin a speakers' series; and the buildings-and-grounds committee requested funds to plant a large flower garden on the property. These were but a few of many items that reflected the vibrant nature of this congregation. The publication contained the names of 88 parishioners serving as members of various committees.

A pledge publication also provides an opportunity for the minister, board chair, and stewardship committee to articulate the important role that stewardship plays in church and in our lives. Other highly regarded parishioners might also relate a story or anecdote about stewardship in their lives. The tone of the publication should be positive, upbeat, and future-oriented.

Tips for Pledge Publications

I've found it surprisingly difficult to get brief articles from committee chairs. For some, it is a matter of procrastination. Others may not have thought much about next year, let alone the years beyond that. Some chairs will want to meet with their committees before deciding what to write. Others struggle with the task of writing. Stewardship committee members will need to telephone or meet with some committee chairs, take notes, and write the articles themselves.

Many committee chairs have resigned themselves to getting the same amount of money as last year, and cannot envision larger hopes and dreams. What would the committee do if it received an additional $5,000 or $10,000? Encourage committee chairs to larger visions!

Always reserve the right to edit articles for content and length. Eventually, the articles may need to be shortened to fit the design of the publication. I recommend hiring a graphic designer rather than using volunteer design help from the congregation. You don't want to get into a disagreement with a parishioner over personal design preferences.

A Pledge Card Is Needed, Too

I recently visited a church in which pledge cards were placed in small holders on the pew-backs. The card had a series of small boxes indicating the amount one might give per week. The choices were $1, $2, $3, $5, and "other," followed by a line on which the church member could write an amount.

A maxim in fund-raising is "Be careful what you ask for, because you might get it." If you ask for a dollar a week, you are granting parishioners permission to give exactly that—one dollar is an acceptable choice. This card was probably the result of a decision made years (or decades) before and carried into the present. Such a tradition encourages parishioners to give only a pittance to the church.

Many churches use a pledge card and a return envelope. My preference is the #9 remittance envelope. The envelope flap is the same size as the envelope itself. The #9 envelope fits into a standard #10 business envelope. I find the #9 remittance envelope useful for a number of reasons. First, it saves money: Only the envelope needs to be printed rather than a card and a separate envelope. Second, the remittance envelope provides space for a brief message about the church and a range of gift options, and leaves room to add a box that parishioners can check if they would like information about putting the church in their wills or estate plans.

The remittance envelope is also large enough to provide a blank space, which should be preceded by the statement, "My hopes and dreams for this church are . . ." This bit of blank space allows every parishioner to take

ownership of the church's current and future life. The remittance envelope
is an important vehicle in allowing parishioners to express their views. It will
provide the stewardship committee additional information about how stewardship initiatives address the issues identified by people in the pews.

How Much Should the Church Ask For?

Many secular organizations provide a range of gift options. If you wish to
support your alma mater or other cause, the choices on the return envelope
might be $25, $50, $100, $250, $500, and $1,000. Colleges and universities
often include higher-level choices of $2,500, $5,000, $10,000, and even
$25,000.

I believe that gift choices offered to parishioners should reinforce the
concept of generosity as a core religious value. I don't believe specific
dollar amounts accomplish this aim. There are many variations. One that I
prefer lists donor options as:

- A number of families in our congregation tithe—give 10% of their income to the church. I/we would like to join them. Our pledge is $_____.

- I/we cannot tithe right away, but would like to begin a plan to tithe. An
  initial pledge toward this goal is $_____.

- I/we pledge $100 per month to the church, or $1,200. _____.

- I/we will pledge $_____ to the church for the coming year.

Readers will notice there is no mention of a gift per week. While I encourage weekly giving as a *practice* and an integral part of the worship experience, I do not recommend the weekly amount as the *basis* for determining
one's pledge or gift. The church pledge should be based on a percentage of
annual income instead. Let me explain why.

If I pledge $5 per week to my church, that is approximately $250 per
year. Let's say I decide to increase my giving by 10 percent. A 10 percent
increase would be considered very generous in a number of situations. A 10

percent increase in my salary would be a pleasant surprise, indeed. If the consumer price index jumped by 10 percent, this would be cause for alarm.

But if I increase my pledge by 10 percent per week, that would be only 10 percent of five dollars, or 50 cents. I would then be pledging $5.50 per week, or $275 per year. Using the weekly amount as the basis of giving allows parishioners to believe they are making generous increases while in fact the total amount given each year can remain very low.

How many congregations would ask parishioners to put $20, $50, or $100 in the Sunday collection—week after week throughout the year? Not many, I suspect. But this is the level at which middle-class families should be giving. By making the tithe the first choice on the return envelope and the plan to tithe the second choice, we are in fact talking about $50 and $100 in the collection plate. Set your sights high, and encourage parishioners to give in relation to their total income.

Let's view the weekly gift from another perspective. Spending $50 for dinner in a restaurant on Saturday night may seem reasonable, even inexpensive in some places. But putting $50 in the collection plate the very next morning would be considered far too great an amount for most Saturday-night diners. The difference in perspective is one that involves the psychology of money. Most people do not think of money in weekly terms. Middle-class churchgoers are not paid on a weekly basis. People do not know how much their mortgage costs on a weekly basis, or their car payment, or their phone bill. A monthly mortgage payment of $1,200 may seem reasonable to many middle-class churchgoers. But that $1,200 monthly payment is $300 per week, which sounds much higher.

Churches are among the few organizations that deal with money on a weekly basis. Stewardship programs should emphasize weekly offerings in a positive way, to reinforce the tradition of giving as part of the worship experience. Don't let stewardship methods inadvertently reinforce the belief that small offerings on Sunday morning are acceptable, even admirable.

I know a minister who announces the offering by saying that one-dollar bills will not accomplish the important work of the congregation—what is required are $20, $50, and $100 bills. Remember, some people will give what you ask them for. Old traditions that limit charitable giving need to fade away. New traditions should be introduced.

The Tenth and 11th Months

By now, the pledge drive will be drawing near. The newsletter has carried upbeat articles from the minister, the stewardship committee, and lay leaders about the upcoming Kickoff Sunday, and the important role that stewardship plays in the lives of all congregants.

The pledge publication and return envelope have been printed by this time. I recommend hand-delivering the publication and pledge card to the top 20 to 25 donors in the congregation, or to those who pledge above a certain amount, maybe $2,500. This is not a visit to solicit a gift! A call saying you'd like to stop by and leave the pledge bulletin that is hot off the press will bring a positive response. The top donors care deeply about the church and wish to see it prosper. They will be curious about the pledge bulletin, and will welcome opportunities to be involved in the life of the congregation.

A cardinal rule of fund-raising is that people give to people. You or members of the stewardship committee, a respected lay leader, or a peer or colleague of the donor can add an important personal touch by making a brief visit. On a strictly pragmatic note, these top donors account for a large portion of the church's total income. Your job is to ensure that they renew or increase their gifts. This is a high priority.

Kickoff Sunday

A newsletter article and pulpit announcements should encourage parishioners not to skip this important event at church. As we have discussed, Kickoff Sunday and the stewardship sermon are not pitches for money. They are important elements in deepening one's spiritual life, in becoming more generous people, and in understanding more fully how God wishes us to share what we have been given.

The mood of Kickoff Sunday should be festive and upbeat. Balloons, refreshments, special music, and a reception following the service will help create an enjoyable atmosphere. People should feel good about being at church, and you want them to stay afterward. Of course the stewardship sermon will be memorable, in part because the stewardship committee has worked so closely with the minister. After the service, committee members should distribute the pledge publication to all who attend. This is most easily done by enclosing the publication and remittance envelope in a larger envelope labeled with the person's name. Handing someone an envelope with his or her name on it adds the personal touch. Envelopes should be distributed on two consecutive Sundays. The remaining envelopes can be mailed to parishioners' homes.

Are Home Visits Necessary?

I believe stewardship programs of any kind are about much more than raising money. They also offer opportunities to check in with each member household. The stewardship campaign is like a thermometer, measuring the temperature and health of the congregation. Stewardship volunteers who visit parishioners' homes will hear candid views about the church, the minister, and how things are going overall. I recommend every-member visits whenever possible.

However, visiting every household in the congregation requires a large number of volunteers. Stewardship committees usually prefer assigning a volunteer (or a two-person team of volunteers) to visit three or four households at most. Visiting every household requires from one-fourth to one-third of the membership. Many congregations are unable to sustain this level of volunteer commitment. Some congregations attempt to visit a percentage of households each year. This approach might be more feasible, but it may also be difficult to sustain if leadership of the stewardship committee changes, along with the visiting policy.

Even if it is possible to recruit one-third of the congregation to make household visits, a number of concerns arise. By involving one-third of the congregation, it will be necessary to reach into the ranks of lower-level donors. This is not a good policy. It is also important for the minister, board members, and stewardship volunteers to understand clearly the purpose of the visit. In many congregations, the purpose is to ask for a gift or pledge. If the intention is to challenge parishioners to lead more generous lives and to reexamine their attitudes toward the acquisition of consumer goods, the purpose of the visit changes dramatically. Volunteers may feel uncomfortable making such calls. Conducting such a stewardship conversation will require a more intensive level of volunteer orientation and training. Also, volunteers who visit fellow parishioners cannot ask people to do what they themselves have not done. This factor may limit the number of visitors available.

One option is visiting the top 20 percent of donors in the congregation. This number of households is likely to be a manageable size. These generous donors should be visited by those of equal giving stature. This system helps ensure that the most generous donors continue to be an integral part of the life of the church community.

Raising money is not a democratic process. We may all be equal in the sight of God, but some people have more money than others, and some have considerably more. The stewardship committee cannot accomplish its work by focusing on low-level donors. It may appear elitist to emphasize higher-level donors, but 80 percent of the money needed to operate the church comes from this group. Until giving increases from all segments of the congregation, the top 20 percent of donors cannot be overlooked. Occasionally you may hear someone say, "If one family gives $1,000 and another family gives only $50, the family that gives more will make the other family feel bad." Do not let this sentiment take root in your congregation. The last thing you want is a generous donor believing that he or she has done the wrong thing!

The Sundays After the Kickoff

If possible, members of the stewardship committee or other respected church members should make brief announcements for the next few Sunday mornings about the benefits of leading more generous lives. If not, the minister should mention stewardship initiatives that are underway. In my own church we planned the pledge drive to include a Sunday service in which the children's choir sang, and attendance was expected to be higher than usual. The stewardship committee offered doughnuts to all children whose parents had turned in their pledge cards. (Of course, all the kids got doughnuts, but a large number asked their parents if they had made their pledges!)

I encourage stewardship representatives to be visible and active during these few weeks by attending all worship services, keeping in touch with parishioners, and cheerfully presenting the case for effective stewardship.

Reporting the Results

Regular updates about the progress of the stewardship campaign should be included in the church newsletter. This is most effectively done in churches that have weekly newsletters. If your church mails newsletters less frequently, consider printing a weekly summary for distribution at church or whenever you feel you have something to report. This update is especially important if pledges are increasing and a sense of momentum is in the air. People like to give to a successful effort, so let them know the favorable outcome.

Know When to Conclude

After a few weeks the highest donors and a sizable number of mid-level donors will have made their commitments. Parishioners who have not pledged are those who attend worship services less frequently and who may not read the church newsletter as regularly. Thus, repeated announcements or newsletter columns addressed to parishioners who have not pledged are ineffective. Do not harangue nondonors from the pulpit or in the newsletter. It is extraordinarily discouraging to parishioners who pledged early to hear repeatedly about those who did not. Avoid this offense at all costs. Do not emphasize the negative. The stewardship committee should contact nondonor households directly by phone or mail, or both.

My hope, of course, is that all the good work preceding the pledge drive has brought an increase in giving or, at the very least, an amount similar to last year's. This outcome will ensure that the church is supported financially for the coming year, and that thoughtful and engaging stewardship initiatives will continue. Remember that pledges will continue to come in throughout the church year.

However, if there is a decrease in giving from the previous year among the earliest pledges, the church leadership should be notified immediately. The stewardship committee does not bear sole responsibility for the success or failure of the annual pledge drive. If parishioners are giving less, the reason is probably not the stewardship committee. They are more likely to be concerned about other aspects of church life. It is the responsibility of the church leadership to undertake an assessment, with the stewardship committee's help, to determine why giving has decreased. This assessment would be similar to the one the leadership conducts in the case of any other church program that had not met expectations.

Acknowledging Gifts and Pledges

See chapter 7, "An Idea That Worked Well," for a recommendation on proper acknowledgment of gifts and pledges.

The Twelfth Month

The final month of the stewardship year is the summing up. The steward-ship committee should report the latest results of the annual pledge drive to the congregation. This includes, at a minimum, the list of gifts and pledges at each level; the increases or decreases in pledging households; the extent of same-level and nonpledging households; the average gift; and the median gift.

By this time parishioners who pledged or made gifts to the church have been thanked appropriately. The stewardship committee should also ex-press its thanks for the support of the minister, the church board, and other key leaders or parishioners.

Also use this opportunity to summarize what members of the steward-ship committee have learned through their efforts to create a congregation of generous people, and how the work has aided their own spiritual growth. It is also important to say that much remains to be discussed. The conversa-tions about how we use money in church and in our lives have been fasci-nating, and will continue into next year and the years beyond.

My hope is that leading stewardship programs has created an enthusi-asm in you and others to continue working toward creating a congregation of generous people. Continuity in leadership is important.

Report Intangibles, Too

While not a part of the stewardship committee's responsibilities per se, you might encourage the minister and church leaders to determine other dimen-sions in which the congregation has grown in faith during the past year. How do new members feel about being part of this religious community?

In what ways has the church called each of us to live more spiritual lives? How has our faith manifested itself in church and in the larger world? Have parishioners been more willing to teach Sunday school? Are the numbers of hours volunteered to the church increasing? Are there memorable moments that parishioners might relate to the congregation that demonstrate a growing faith, or the presence of God at church or in their everyday lives?

These issues are integral to creating meaningful religious lives. Stewardship, along with the various ways in which churches raise money, is not separate from the life of the congregation. Rather, these are part of the fabric of church life, woven into what God calls us to do, and how we respond. I hope you take great pride in what you have accomplished.

NOTES

Preface

1. Robert Wuthnow, *The Crisis in the Churches: Spiritual Malaise, Fiscal Woe* (New York: Oxford University Press, 1997).
2. Loren Mead, *Financial Meltdown in the Mainline?* (Bethesda: Alban Institute, 1998).
3. Deborah Milton, "A Class Act Institute," *Stewardship Matters: The Magazine of the Christian Stewardship Association,* 2, no. 1 (1999): 15.

Chapter 1

1. Lyle Schaller, *44 Ways to Expand the Financial Base of Your Congregation* (Nashville: Abingdon, 1989), 144.
2. Clark Hargus, *Biblical Stewardship Principles* (Indianapolis: Ecumenical Center for Stewardship Studies, 1991).
3. Juliet Schor, *The Overspent American* (New York: Basic Books, 1998), 12-13.
4. Eileen Daspin, "How to Give More," *Wall Street Journal,* 2 October 1998, W1.
5. Scott Cormode, "Raising Funds by the Good Book," *Chronicle of Philanthropy,* 17 (June 1999): 37.
6. Tom Beaudoin, *Virtual Faith: The Irreverent Spiritual Quest of Generation X* (San Francisco: Jossey Bass, 1998), xiv.
7. Dean Hoge, Patrick McNamara, and Charles Zech, *Plain Talk About Churches and Money* (Bethesda: Alban Institute, 1997), 52.

8. Beaudoin, *Virtual Faith,* xvi.

9. Anthony Pappas, *Money, Motivation, and Mission in the Small Church* (Valley Forge: Judson, 1989), 45.

10. Tom McCabe, "Understanding the Ministry of Fundraising," *Stewardship Matters,* 1, no. 1 (1999): 7.

Chapter 2

1. In many Jewish synagogues, members are assessed dues. The amount an individual or family is assessed depends on age, size of family, and income. In most synagogues dues are considerably higher than the giving expectations in mainline Christian churches.

2. Ashley Hale, *The Lost Art of Church Fund-Raising* (Chicago: Precept Press, 1993). The BPATG is taken from an article by Hale, and draws on his 50 years of church fund-raising experience summarized in this delightful book.

3. Taylor Branch, *Parting the Waters: America in the King Years, 1954-1963* (New York: Simon & Schuster, 1988), 41-42.

4. Mead, *Financial Meltdown,* 105.

5. Mead, *Financial Meltdown,* 105.

6. Edward Landreth, *Fund-Raising With a Vision* (Boston: Unitarian Universalist Association, 1997), 20.

7. Robert Wood Lynn, "Why Give?" in *Financing American Religion* (Walnut Creek, Calif.: AltaMira Press, 1999), 55.

8. Lyle Schaller, *The Middle-Sized Church* (Nashville: Abingdon, 1985), 33-64. Schaller devotes an entire chapter to the idea that no two congregations are alike.

Chapter 3

1. Mark Chaves and Sharon Miller, eds., *Financing American Religion* (Walnut Creek, Calif.: AltaMira Press, 1999). All quotations are used with permission of the authors.

2. Mark Chaves, "Financing American Religion," in *Financing American Religion,* 172.

3. Sharon L. Miller, "The Meaning of Religious Giving," in *Financing American Religion,* 41.

4. Chaves, "Financing," in *Financing American Religion, 178.*

5. Laurent Park Daloz, *Can Generosity Be Taught?*, Essays on Philanthropy, no. 29 (Indianapolis: Indiana University, 1988), 6.

6. Victor Claman, *Acting on Your Faith: Congregations Making a Difference* (Boston: Insights Press, 1997).

7. Kennon Callahan, *Giving and Stewardship in an Effective Church* (San Francisco: Harper Books, 1992), 3.

8. Douglas John Hall, *The Steward: A Biblical Symbol Come of Age* (Grand Rapids: Eerdmans, 1990), 13.

9. Hall, *The Steward*, 15.

10. Miller, "Meaning," in *Financing American Religion*, 38.

11. Miller, "Meaning," in *Financing American Religion,* 42.

12. Chaves, "Financing," in *Financing American Religion,* 178.

Chapter 4

1. John and Sylvia Ronsvalle, *Behind the Stained Glass Windows: Money Dynamics in the Church* (Grand Rapids: Baker Books, 1996), 31.

2. Robert Randall, *What People Expect from Church* (Nashville: Abingdon, 1992), 21.

3. Hall, *The Steward*, 13.

4. Carolyn Clarke, from the bylaws of First Baptist Church, Belmont, Mass.

5. Peter Gomes, *The Good Book* (New York: William Morrow, 1996), 287.

6. Gomes, *The Good Book*, 286.

7. Charles Jaffee, "Financial Planning for the Year Ahead," *Boston Globe,* 3 January 1997.

Chapter 5

1. Hale, *The Lost Art*, 78.

2. Schaller, *Middle-Sized Church*, 105.

3. Schaller, *Middle-Sized Church,* 105.

4. Pappas, *Money, Motivation, and Mission*, 11.

5. Hale, *The Lost Art*, 78.

6. H. Richard Niebuhr, *The Social Sources of Denominationalism* (Gloucester, Mass.: Peter Smith, 1980), 104-105.

Chapter 6

1. Loren Mead, "Caught in the Financial Bind: Reflections on Clergy and Money," *Congregations: The Alban Journal* (July-August 1996): 3.
2. Mead, "Caught in the Financial Bind," 3.
3. Hall, *The Steward*, 13.
4. Daniel Conway, "Clergy as Reluctant Stewards," in *Financing,* ed. Chavez and Miller, 96.
5. Conway, "Clergy as Reluctant Stewards," 98.
6. Schaller, *44 Ways*, 113-164.

Chapter 7

1. Schaller, *44 Ways,* 167-168.
2. Hall, *The Steward*, 14.
3. Don McLanen, "What You Have in Comparison to Others," *Ministry of Money Newsletter,* February 1999.

Chapter 8

1. Hale, *The Lost Art,* 52.
2. Hale, *The Lost Art,* 54.
3. Joseph Harmon, *Philanthropy in Short Fiction,* Essays on Philanthropy, no.6 (Indianapolis: Indiana University, 1991), 1-2.
4. Stephen Carter, *The Culture of Disbelief* (New York: Basic Books, 1993), 3-4.
5. Wuthnow, *Crisis.* These themes are discussed throughout this important work.
6. Ronsvalle and Ronsvalle, *Behind the Stained Glass Windows*, 35.
7. Wuthnow, *Crisis*, 7-8.